HOME TRUTHS

A JAUNT AROUND THE DECAYING HEART OF ENGLAND

BILL MURPHY

MAINSTREAM
PUBLISHING

EDINBURGH AND LONDON

First published in Great Britain in 2000 by
MAINSTREAM PUBLISHING COMPANY (EDINBURGH) LTD
7 Albany Street
Edinburgh EH1 3UG

ISBN 1 84018 331 4

Typeset in Garamond
Printed and bound in Great Britain by Creative Print and Design Wales

To Robert Bruce

Contents

Introduction

The aim of this book is to document the irreversible destruction that has occurred across much of urban England and the English countryside, and the knock-on effects this has had on its people.

There appears to be some mysterious convention whereby neither authors nor broadcasters can describe England as it really is. Only newspaper columnists can touch on the rampant decay that has permeated the nation over the last 20 years. Even then they do so either to heads that nod passively or to the argument that *every* civilisation enters an inevitable state of decay sooner or later.

Overwhelmingly, travel writers at best seem merely to touch on the unpleasant nature of English towns, and at worst do so armed with a barrage of excuses and apologies for bringing up the subject in the first place.

I wanted to go out into the provinces and paint a picture of just how dreadful England has become. This was to involve seeing those places first hand, and mixing with the kind of people who enjoy the National Lottery, football and BBC fly-on-the-wall documentaries. I wanted to meet the people who make *Noel's House Party* so popular. In the event, what startled me was the sheer scale of the new English underclass; in some cases I saw entire towns made up of people of little or no use to any employer. By 'underclass' I mean the generation that has given up on society, not the traditional working class.

I set out to tour towns and cities of England and describe just how moribund they have all become. I don't expect for one minute that there won't be outcries from various quarters, not least the Third World, whose peoples will probably want to take a swipe at me for likening it to Stoke-on-Trent. All I know is that I spent long enough in each locality to develop a clear sense of what it was like.

Incidentally, if you think I am being unfairly biased towards London, you've obviously only ever read about the place in a book. It's one hell of a sight safer than out in the sticks. The centres of Southampton, Coventry, Wolverhampton, Sunderland, Birmingham, Bristol – the list goes on; in terms of crime they are all now deemed by insurance companies to be a substantially greater risk than virtually any part of the capital.

I set about this project early in 1999 and spent a gruelling eight months acquainting myself with over 30 English towns and cities that, my research had told me, would stand up to the charge of decay. None of them let me down.

The task meant I had to meet the population that makes up the teacher-driven excuse society. It also meant witnessing how much of the country has been physically destroyed by bogus homes erected in the past two decades. It was painful.

The only conclusion I can draw is that things can only get worse – unless (as seldom happens today) someone occasionally stops to think about what consequences his actions and decisions may have in 50 or 150 years' time. It seems a tragedy if all we can do is destroy the pleasanter legacies of the past and leave none for the future.

1. Braintree

The ugliest collection of people in the UK outside Wales

A couple of million years ago, the eastern regions of the British Isles as we now know them were situated below sea level. It is just a shame that when ice ages caused fluctuations in the depth of the surrounding sea and East Anglia joined the rest of the island, it had to drag Essex along with it. There is still hope, I suppose, with the promise of global warming that is said to be just around the corner, but it does mean having to wait to see what results its associated rising tides can bring.

Supporting such geological assertions is the core population of the area, which seems to be a lot closer to sea life than the rest of England. A good number of its female inhabitants in particular resemble sea monsters.

Braintree is only an hour's train ride east of London, so on arriving there I didn't feel like I was at the end of a particularly long journey. However, when I stepped out of the station and on to the streets of Braintree, I did feel as if I'd reached the end of the food chain.

To many, the town is best known for its unmarried pregnant mothers, and visitors are encouraged to try and spot wedding rings on the hands of local young women with pushchairs. It can't often be done. And it should not be assumed that there is an army of local industrious teenage babysitters. There isn't.

The high street is fascinating. Like Wales, most of it seems either closed down or broken. It has just one department store – this in a town of over 50,000 – called Town Row, which looks like a cross between an abandoned 1920s Methodist church and a charity store. Above it is a naked flagmast. Sadly, the only people to have flown a flag in Braintree for some considerable time have been wearing shirts made from 100 per cent manmade fibres bearing the name of either a Japanese electronics manufacturer or some European brewery.

Opposite Town Row was a photograph-framing centre which had clearly seen better days – or had it? One picture on display appeared at first glance to be that of a moose which had recently escaped from somewhere like Colchester Zoo. But then I noticed she had tattoos on her front legs and was wearing a mini-skirt.

It was closing time for the shops. The manager of an adjacent shop had pulled down the metal grille and was locking it up. He was clad in shorts and a white vest. But my alarm at this was knocked for six when the first pair of trainers I'd ever seen with attached stiletto heels walked past, supporting a mini-skirted twenty-something girl. The burden in her womb was causing her to lean at a precarious angle.

Braintree's bookstore had on display in its front window many copies of a book on Braintree and its surroundings which had all mysteriously been greatly reduced in price. Not heard of it? You'll find it in any good bookshop. In Braintree.

Braintree is a town with no particular industry and therefore nothing to generate revenue, which means there is virtually nothing in the way of wealth. The place is a retreat largely for inhabitants of dives on the fringe of London such as Dagenham and Deptford, who wish to exist alongside others on a similar point on the evolutionary scale but who 'don't want to be surrounded any longer by non-Caucasian illegal immigrants'. At least that's what I was told by all those half-dozen or so inhabitants I asked.

The town is great for sightseeing. My first sight was of a representative cross-section of the local population near the town square: eight people were seated on three benches and going about their daily business. They were, first of all, three scantily clad girls of about 15 years of age playing truant, smoking and eyeing up each male that came within their radar zone. Next were two village idiots dressed even more badly than the rest of those living in the district. One of them had a plimsoll on one foot and a slipper on the other. Beside them on the next bench was an elderly couple out enjoying the sunshine and sharing their seat with two empty wine bottles. Next to them sat a woman in a grubby purple sleeveless T-shirt, swigging a bottle of wine and cackling quietly to herself. She could have been anything between about 16 and 60. Probably the latter, as she didn't seem pregnant. Across the road, or rather on the other side of the pedestrianised walkway, was what I assumed to be a local insurance broker: Hush Puppies, mobile phone, notebook computer, dirty fawn raincoat.

As I stood and absorbed all this, two girls of about 14 and clad in a kind of bespoke school uniform passed by, discussing the younger one's current predicament. 'If I was to miscarriage – if I was to miscarriage, right – and my mum found out, right . . .' Her words faded as she turned off to the right.

But the town does have its snobs. I spotted the Constitution Club by the market square and tried to gain entry. In my most sincere tones I lied, claiming that I was a Lloyd's underwriter visiting from London and that I assumed the only half-decent place to drink in Braintree was that particular establishment. The doorman shook his head. I don't think he was impressed by my denim jacket.

The next level of class in Braintree down from there is a sharp plummet on the evolutionary scale and can be found occupying and running a few bars which deem themselves to be exclusive of low life. One of these is the White Hart. Its Executive Bar, which was shut, resembled a village hall. All it lacked were trays of sandwiches on the tables.

I had already booked into another, cheaper-looking hotel in the high street, but I was curious to know how much this place charged. A girl at the reception hatch showed me the price list. I declined the offer of a room at £40 a night, using the excuse that I was asthmatic and would be affected by paint fumes. The whole place was in the process of being redecorated.

But I climbed over a fallen ladder, dust sheets and paint cans to at least visit the hotel's main bar, which was empty, where I found myself unable to order a cup of coffee, strictly forbidden for sale as it was between 10 a.m. and 5 p.m. So I bought a pint from the barman, who also appeared to be the manager of the place. I enquired about other pubs in the area, and he said there was nowhere but his hotel to drink safely. He knew – he had lived here all his life. In the background an album of instrumental covers of hits by various artists from the mid-1980s was playing.

'It's a dismal place, isn't it?' I said.

'This hotel?'

'No, Braintree.'

'Braintree? Oh *God* yes,' he said, before thankfully declining my offer of a drink.

I asked for some literature which would describe the inn itself, and an assistant barmaid produced a booklet of inns around the UK. The White Hart was featured on page 69, she said. I thanked her, sat down and tore out the relevant page before returning the booklet.

I asked the manager again where I might best go for a taste of Braintree life and its people. I was the only person in the bar, presumably because nobody else locally had the initiative to find his way over the obstacle course of decorating materials. He advised me, 'Stay here, have a few drinks, a three-course meal, then stay in the bar till eleven.'

I reminded him again of the purpose of the visit.

'No, seriously, people come to Braintree, they nearly all stay here, and they stay in the bar till eleven o'clock. Seriously. That's the God's honest truth,' he said. 'Seriously, they spend loads of money, because I've persuaded them.'

For some reason I found myself retreating faster than I would have done normally. I left to the sound of him pleading, 'No, honestly, you might as well stay here all night . . .' A desperate man. On my way out I heard him lower his voice and say to the barmaid, 'We won't see *him* again till next Christmas.' So I stuck my head back round the door to reassure him I'd have other plans over the festive season.

As I left the hotel I saw a boy of about ten standing in the middle of the road and throwing an open plastic soft-drink bottle high up in the air so it would land and spray the surrounding area with its contents. Probably the only child in Braintree to throw coke away.

The town centre's streets are all lined with video cameras and in the high street is a large warning sign to this effect. The *Braintree Evening Gazette* ran a story that day about an ongoing court case involving a married couple accused of petrol-bombing their former employer's taxi business. This had allegedly been caught on video. The trial was continuing.

The *Evening Gazette* is not short of stories about car thefts, and if its reports are to be believed, the courts are clogged up with a backlog of cases of young men arrested for drunken brawls. The *Braintree Times*, meanwhile, carried five stories that day in its news-in-brief section: windows were smashed at a Braintree high school; vandals had scratched the paintwork of a Fiat; vandals – it didn't say whether they were the same ones – had smashed up a greenhouse in Braintree; thieves had failed with an attempted house break-in; and a Vauxhall Nova had been stolen in Braintree and later set on fire. The locals, I noted, were nothing if not industrious.

Adjacent to that column was a story which reflected the low expectations of people in that part of the world:

> Readers are getting the chance to make history and star in
> the millennium experience. Dome chiefs want people to
> send in photos of themselves, their families and friends
> for a massive multi-coloured collage of British life.

Big deal.

For such a large surrounding population there is remarkably little in the way of town-centre activities such as pubs and cinemas. The locals blame the police. The police in turn produce reports defending their decisions not to allow, for instance, cinemas to stay open late, as 'officers will have to work late'. One such report appeared in that day's *Evening Chronicle*.

In the late Middle Ages the unpopular office of Parish Constable – an unpaid year-long duty meted out to parish residents much in the manner of jury duty – gave way to that of semi-professional constables who would hold the post for several years. According to *The Essex Police* by John Woodgate (Terrence Dalton Ltd, 1985), 'many of these "professional" constables were unintelligent, generally inefficient and always the cheapest available'. So, no change there.

Braintree is home to the most neurotic breed of women, and it's hardly surprising, A significant proportion of them are from east and north London's poorest districts and come with attitude problems. Or so I was told by Dave, a friendly enough guy I spoke to in the Kings Arms.

'I knew someone who was murdered in the town recently,' he volunteered when he heard I was writing about the place. 'Me and some lads were walking through the high street. Some young lads came up, split us up, and a bloke – a stranger – walked up and knifed this guy in the back. All you get round here is a load of pissheads.'

He too cursed the police for preventing any commercial evening initiatives – such as nightclubs – from succeeding. 'Every time something opens, the Old Bill closes it down,' he lamented. He then explained that the population of over 50,000 was mostly centred in three large 'estates' on the edge of the town. Glebe Estate, he said, was made up of north London tattooed and beer-gutted slobs. Fairview Estate he described as 'middle class', and Goldingham comprised thousands of east London cropped-hair Lahn-dan-accented 'Cockney wankers' whose only expertise apart from car-breaking and drug-dealing was 'hoddying', which he explained meant carrying bricks on a building site.

I remarked that there seemed to be an unusually high number of girls with tattoos. 'I love 'em!' he replied as his tattooed girlfriend came in and ordered Braintree woman's drink: sweet white wine and lemonade.

I thanked him and left, taking a cab back to the town centre, where I went to one of the two clubs – which was in fact a pub with a licence to trade till midnight. The girl behind the bar was 19 and had lived in Braintree for the past ten years, so, deducing that she must have attended school in the area, I asked her what it was like. 'Didn't go very often. Don't know,' she replied. She had left school for good when she was 13.

Behind her, alongside the optics, was a sign much in the style of those which warn against the use of drugs in other municipalities. It gave a flavour of what to expect in Braintree:

> The Braintree and District Licensed Victuallers Association announce that any person convicted of assault on a publican, his wife, family or staff, or Police Officers in the exercise of their duty, will be barred from all licensed premises under Braintree LVA membership.

I wondered why 'police officers' should have been capitalised.

To the left of the bar was a cigarette machine which looked unusual at first glance. On closer inspection I realised I really *hadn't* seen one like it before: its main feature was a broad and unseemly metal security bar across the front which was bolted on to either side. Presumably a necessary precaution in the district.

I tried to work out what it was that made Braintree such an absolute shithole, apart from the obvious attributes it had – a population which originated more or less exclusively in what Steve Coogan playing the part of Alan Partridge once described as 'the maggot-ridden cess pit that is the East End of London'. In actual fact the town is laid out very much like Stoke-on-Trent (see chapter 21). Both have small town centres, and both service a handful of massive housing estates. But Stoke's residents aren't prevented from enjoying themselves with a bit of variety because, unlike Braintree, not everything is closed down by the police, as my friend claimed happened regularly in Braintree.

I looked around the venue. On a neighbouring bar stool was a village idiot. I caught his eye and it stared back at me, forcing me to cross to the far end of the bar. Doing so I sensed I was setting foot in my first Club 18–70 experience.

As the evening dragged on I became hungry and left to find a restaurant. I saw a packed Wimpy whose location I noted in case I should need it later. The two Indian restaurants were takeaway only. I stopped and chatted to one of the members of staff standing out on the street, Ali, who showed me the balti menu. It looked tempting, but I was not prepared to stand on the streets of Braintree eating curry with a plastic fork.

Ali told me what I had already deduced: that there is not a great deal of money in Braintree. 'I learned this soon after buying the shop,' he said sadly. He also soon learned of the severe drought in Braintree when it comes to manners. Ali was about the only polite and courteous individual I was to meet there. Indeed, I saw no more in the way of good manners there than I saw of people smiling. Almost everyone's expression was grim, except for the few young girls on the pull who were yet to become mothers. Braintree really did appear to hold the most humourless collection of people outside Germany.

I eventually found a pizza restaurant, which I concluded must have been the only eating place in the area where one could sit down. I walked in to 'wait to be seated' and was pushed past by a family of three. A few hours in Braintree had taught me to expect that.

But then I noticed they were in fact German. We were seated at adjacent tables. Minutes later the astute waitress, who identified me as having been first in the queue, asked, 'Are you ready to order?' and I replied in the affirmative. This was too much for the German father, who said in irony-free monotones, 'Ve are ready to order.' Thankfully the waitress ignored him. This must have infuriated him, a member of the master race.

At the front of the restaurant were six girls of around 18 – tarts, the lot of them. They were all as eager for male attention as the rest. Their conversation, though loud, was, believe it or not, on a slightly higher intellectual level than most to which I'd been exposed that day. Some of them even managed to assemble three-clause, intelligible sentences; for instance, 'When you go for 'em, go for their balls – it unnerves 'em!', followed by a raucous and high-pitched noise from all six of them such as you would hear in a bird sanctuary. There may have been plenty of tottie there but Braintree was certainly not a bird sanctuary.

A minute later I looked up over my spaghetti bolognese and

saw the fattest amongst them eyeing me up. In fact I had never been eyed up by so many women in my life as in those long, dark hours in Braintree. This was to no avail, of course – I am married. Sorry, girls, 'fat, balding, unshaven and bespectacled Bill Murphy' (Welsh *Mirror*, 26 July 1999) is spoken for.

However, I am human, and my eyes shot out as though on stalks when a girl passed by my table in a short, tight skirt and a silk top which paid lip-service to the role of covering her breasts. This, I discovered, was the manageress.

I paid the bill and left a tip which brought amazement to the face of the cashier, and returned to the town centre to find another bar. By now I was feeling wretched and unhappy.

The last recession which officially ended in 1992 brought distress to much of England and was talked of as being 'current' for a further three years by many small businessmen. However, five years later, recovery has more or less permeated the country, although of course businesses continue to fold at their usual inter-recession rate. Braintree is an exception. It has never recovered and looks as if it never will. I can only assume the reason is that the place is such a dive, with such a shabby and dangerous population, that anyone with capital to invest has avoided it.

I hadn't realised, when my friend Simon persuaded me that I would have to include Braintree if I was to write a truly definitive study of the arse end of England, that he was playing such a cruel practical joke.

Even the hotel, run by an ex-merchant seaman who did not come from Braintree, pandered to the low level of expectation which prevails in the town. All its floors creaked and lay at different angles to each other. The bedroom itself was of an impossibly awkward layout. It had one power point, so when I wanted to recharge my phone the lights went out. The ensuite bathroom had an unusable shower and a sink the size of a large soup bowl with a 1950s pipe which produced water from a bucket-sized tank. Very Wormwood Scrubs. But the landlord seemed charming, helpful and was not without a sense of humour.

At the end of the evening – when, by 10.30, I had suffered more than I considered reasonable and wanted to retreat to type up the day's observations – I returned to the hotel, only to find the front door locked. I rang the bell several times during the next ten minutes to no answer. My mobile didn't seem to work so I memorised the phone number on the note beside the door to be used in the event of no answer, went back to the pub and rang it. I was put through to a mobile phone answering service.

Unsure what exactly to do, and by this time being a little pissed, I stayed in the pub. I bought a Coke, found a payphone and for £1.20 had a 20-second conversation with my wife in London, during which she advised me to come home. I was able to say the words 'a', 'cab' and 'costs' before it cut out, causing her to miss the words '65' and 'quid'.

Half an hour of slowly sipping Coke later, during which time I witnessed a highly competitive game of tattooed-women's darts, I sidled back to the hotel. It was 11.15 p.m., and the landlord was fortunately just returning from his evening's work as a minicab driver. I told him I'd been unable to get in. He shrugged and said the door was open now, which indeed it was. Thanking him coldly, I went on up to my uncomfortable bed and lay with the high street's lights beaming on me through the thin curtains.

My 8.30 a.m. call never materialised. I got up when I awoke at nine, dressed and packed and went downstairs for breakfast. All the doors were locked, so I picked up my bags and went to find the landlord elsewhere in the building so I could pay and get out of Braintree altogether.

'Have some breakfast,' he suggested when at last I found him. But I wanted to get out of there, and fast.

I went instead to find a café. It was here that I discovered it is established Braintree practice not even to acknowledge other patrons at a table with unoccupied seats, let alone to ask them if the seats are taken. I shared my table with an elderly lady who joined me to sip at a mug of coffee and watch me eat my bacon and eggs.

I expect it was uncustomary Braintree behaviour, but I paid for my meal, before heading off for the library. I stepped inside, passed through the machine-gun nests, and there ahead of me was about half an acre of crowded floor space. So I was wrong – there are plenty of literate people in Braintree. This was a revelation. Or at least it would have been but for the fact that, through the crowds, I saw shelves containing not books but video and audio cassettes. I wandered around looking for books but could find not one.

I was about to leave when I noticed a stairway. I walked up it and found myself in a sparsely furnished open-plan room. At the far end was a series of half a dozen miniature shelving units, which I approached. This was where I was to find the books. The rest of the floor had four or so tables and a desk around which the librarians themselves were chatting.

I picked up a book on Braintree which was to turn out to be as bland as I expected and sat down to read it. A moment later my mobile phone rang. A finger in my other ear to block out the sound of the conversations of the nearby librarians who were themselves blocking out those of the somewhat quieter town gossips, I answered it in a semi-whisper.

A few seconds later a spotty, bespectacled youth in a shirt and tie approached me and told me to turn it off. 'We don't allow mobile phones in here,' he explained. I obliged, deciding against an argument concerning the definition of multi-media. And besides, it had turned 11 a.m. and the pubs were open.

I bought a pint and sat down to read the local paper. A moment later a guy I recognised from the night before approached me and asked how the book was coming along.

'Okay. How're you doing?' I asked.

'In court today,' he said, with a grin.

'Best of luck,' I said. Unbelievable. Still, at least he was now wearing a shirt.

Still smarting from the attitude of the hotel proprietor and depressed out of my mind by the location and its inhabitants, I resolved to ring my friend Simon to ask him to come as soon as he could to drive me back to London as he had promised – part of the deal under which I would come and write a study of Braintree.

I could get no mobile phone signal in the pub so I stepped outside. I had to keep the conversation brief because a woman standing two yards away began to shout at and then to attack a traffic warden who had stuck a parking ticket on her car. Pregnant, the aggressor had a cigarette in one hand and a baby in the other. As I retreated to the relative safety of the pub, I noticed she had no wedding ring.

Uniformed reinforcements were quick to arrive, and the otherwise stagnant streets were electrified by a sudden crowd gawping at the scene in question. The woman's attitude was fair enough, I thought, for she had only been parked there a couple of minutes and the fine would presumably eat up that week's giro. I noticed every head in the pub was turned to look out of the window (along, admittedly, with my own, but mine was turned purely for research purposes).

The crowd that had gathered concealed from view the actions of the woman but gave me an opportunity to see a wider cross-section of townsfolk than any to which I had so far been treated. Those in scruffy jeans and trainers were the smartest set. Most of them under 65 had tattoos. There was an abundance of girls in stilettos and short skirts. Half the men wore no shirts. Probably the ugliest collection of people in the UK outside Wales.

Pint finished, crowd dispersed and Simon still half an hour from arriving to rescue me, I went to the Oxfam shop. In much the same way as it benefits from the water cycle, Braintree benefits too from its own clothes cycle. The place was mobbed. I had to get the hell out of there, and fast.

Suffice to say, Braintree has no redeeming qualities. If there is anything good about it, it is its proximity to the M11 heading south.

2. Southport

So dead, not even the sea turns up anymore

I took up the offer from Simon to cadge a lift to Southport, where he had to spend a couple of days on business.

I knew nothing of Southport beforehand, although I was told on the way there that it was a famous seaside resort on the north-west, some way north of Liverpool. It seemed to be famous only to those living in the north-west.

I'd never seen that part of the world before – not north of Liverpool, anyway. I'd not missed much either. There's a place called Maghull on the A59 approaching Southport which looks like a giant dunny (*n.* toilet *aus. sl.*). We were caught in a traffic jam caused by abandoned roadworks, which gave me a chance to study the local people. These ones were *ugly*. Not just plain, like the people I was later to encounter in Stevenage, but *hideous*. Fat and miserable-looking. A plump middle-aged woman in a red Ford gave us a look of anger when we reversed to let her into a car park through the line of cars. We'd held her up for a few seconds before she'd had the chance to get through. Add impatient and self-centred to the list.

Once past the roadworks, we sped on through Lydiate and on to agriculturally rich countryside with fields for miles in every direction growing nothing but cabbages. And when I was to arrive in Southport I would meet even more cabbages, in the local Conservative Club. But that's later on in this chapter.

Nearing Southport, in the distance we could see the docks. All that lay between us and them were broken walls and weeds.

A big sign welcomed us to Southport, winner of Britain in Bloom – presumably some time in the last century, as all I could see was a Homebase and a few dying trees. And at last we were in Southport, where every commercial building is either a retirement home or an Italian restaurant. Sorry, ristorante pizzeria. The place looked as if it was run by the mafia; even the diminutive undertakers wore dark glasses (in the rain). And it was unsurprising that the town is predominantly Roman Catholic. The Catholic churches were typically surrounded by scaffolding, suggesting they spend much more time renovating their churches than they do their own houses.

All the cars were either BMWs and Mercedes driven by cloth-capped northerners (go there and see for yourself if you don't believe me) or Ford Capris and Escorts with spoilers, to indicate *class*.

Entering the main street leading down to the seafront (only a mile short of the sea) – or the Promenade, as it's known – we noticed that businesses there diversified. There were still many, many ristorante pizzerias, and quite a few more retirement homes, between the boarded-up hotels and music halls, but colour was added with a sprinkling of tattoo-artist boutiques, amusement arcades and chip shops. The streets in the town centre were lined with what looked like Christmas lights which hadn't been taken down the year before last because nobody could afford to pay someone to remove them.

We had to find somewhere to stay, but finding somewhere that looked as though it might be comfortable was too much of a challenge so we stopped at the first hotel on the 'seafront' we could find that looked better than the norm. It had a condemned and rusty fire escape and didn't appear to have been painted in the 30 years that had passed since it was last in dire need of decoration. The letters of its name had come unhinged from the side of the building, and it fitted perfectly into what Southport really is: a town that in Victorian days was upmarket but for decades has been left to rot. And the fact that the front door could only be opened with the correct five-character changeable alphanumeric code seemed to say something about the need for security in Southport.

The landlady said we were lucky to have caught her. 'I was just off to Morecambe,' she said, before adding hastily, 'for *shopping*.'

We paid up front for the night in rooms on the top floor with ensuite bathrooms, and left to see the town itself. We found a pub with benches outside. On the way there we had passed a church with a hearse waiting outside. Next door to the church was another retirement home, so they had their supplier more or less on their doorstep. Unlike Haverhill in Suffolk (chapter 5), Southport is a retirement home for the genuinely aged.

In the pub across the road, the Windmill, we were greeted with a Southport welcome when we were short-changed by the guy behind the bar, who then looked most vexed that we'd worked out that we were a quid short. Noting the age of visitors, most of whom were at least 60, I guessed this had become a habit among town vendors. It was to happen in other pubs as well, so this comment about short-changing is making it into the book on the grounds of fair comment.

The pub's loo had its own skating facilities courtesy of whoever didn't bother to mop the piss lake off the floor. Yet despite all this, the families having lunch there looked as happy as pigs in shit. So the coastal town of Southport must be as good as it gets in the north-west. All the men we could see were presumably unfortunate factory workers who escaped once a year to this. No wonder they're all so dour. Even the trees, though still alive, were depressed, shedding their leaves in August.

Neighbouring towns describe Southport as 'so dead not even the sea turns up anymore'. When a sea wall was erected a couple of years ago, the shore migrated about a mile further out from what had traditionally been the coast. Southport is therefore an inland coastal town.

I bought the local paper, the *Southport Visiter*, which is how it is in fact spelt. I thought this must have meant something other than visitor, but I saw no evidence of this and just got a complacent 'yeah, "visitor" is spelt wrong – so what?' from those locals I asked. Every couple of pages it had a 'Look who's in court' column. The courts were clearly very busy indeed. I didn't study the front page closely, but imagine that under 'The Visiter' banner were the words 'Mis-spelt since 1884'.

Nearby was a pub called Rueters (*sic*) of Hoghton. We went in and asked if it was named after the Reuters news agency. 'Oh, yes, this building used to be the offices of the *Daily Star*,' the informed barmaid said. It was located in Houghton Street (presumably pronounced 'Huoghton').

On page three of the *Visiter* was a story reporting the forthcoming eclipse. 'Daytime will become night for around two hours,' it explained. Strange that Southport's massively extended eclipse wasn't pulling in any more visiters. The journalist who wrote it had obviously been drinking in Rueters. The paper's dairy page listed forthcoming local events.

Every woman over 16 looked old-aged. Many of them had remarkably large breasts, but sadly their arses and bellies were of proportionate size. Everyone seemed to have big hair, high heels and flares. And nine out of ten women were peroxide blondes. One hundred per cent of these wore gold-coloured stiletto sandals.

We entered an Irish theme bar and, in the style of Celtic writing for the tourist, on the door was a large sign saying 'Please leave the pub quietly'.

Down the road was the 50th ristorante pizzeria we came to. At the entrance were two lion statues on top of plinths, à la Trafalgar Square. The only notable thing about these was that they were facing the wrong way with their backs towards the street. Nearby, the north-facing Sunnyside Court appeared to have been built recently more in hope than expectation.

Further down the road we reached a district where the bottom quarters of all the lamp posts were painted red. Our hopes fell when we discovered this didn't in fact denote the red-light district.

As we headed back into town there was plenty of evidence of bygone times of affluence, with large dilapidated Victorian mansions. Then we saw one which had been renovated and looked in a relatively habitable condition. The effect was somewhat spoiled by a satellite dish proudly located two-thirds of the way up the wall, facing the road. The other buildings around it had been irredeemably wrecked in the 1960s with

garages put in to destroy any chance of restoration. Every so often we'd see a cracked pebbledash building whose owners had aspirations for artificial cladding. Round the corner was something neither of us had ever seen before: a council tower block with a supermarket occupying the ground floor.

Southport has its own way of doing things, and not just with respect to spelling – Hoghton Court, for instance, located in the Houghton district of the town. Here there were parking restrictions which seemed to be begging people not to leave. Instead of 'residents parking only', the parking signs read 'Waiting time restricted to ten hours'.

All the hotel owners had to have been living on the breadline, for since the sea had left, so had most of the tourists. I likened it to Scarborough in December, and not without good cause. A few years earlier I had tried a pilot trip round shit areas of the country with the same purpose of finding out what living in these places must be like. Out-of-season Scarborough was *grim*. The seafront was more or less deserted, with most candyfloss and ice-cream stalls abandoned for the winter. The chip shops were bolted shut, and there was no industry worth speaking of. It was painful to see a population which relied totally on tourism for a living. The only tourists were retired couples revisiting the place they had been every summer holiday since they were engaged 40 or 50 years earlier, for the sake of nostalgia.

I had on that occasion booked into a Scarborough B&B which had set me back ten quid and included a massive breakfast, after which I had left to explore the town. It had been ghostly as well as ghastly, but the locals were putting on a brave face. It was also very eerie to think that virtually everybody I encountered was living on the takings of the previous summer, and that most wouldn't see another penny till the following Easter. I'm surprised that the pubs bothered to open during these months, for the locals clearly couldn't afford to go out. I went into one bar which seemed to be a converted dance hall. I was the only customer that night. The barmaid was not as downcast as she might have been for, despite the lack of customers, she was one of the few who would be receiving an income of sorts during the bleak months of September to July.

Southport itself was not *quite* as dead in August as Scarborough was in early December, but those relying on tourism for a living – which was just about all of them apart from the undertakers – looked miserable, and behaved it too. At first I thought it was redeemed through the absence of grotesque and tacky theme bars. But when we hit the town at around 7 p.m., we found plenty of them in the vicinity of the town hall.

By the end of the trip I was to find only one other place which resembled Southport, and that was Cheltenham (see chapter 20). The shop-lined road resembled Cheltenham's Promenade in just about every respect. The town hall was of a similar vintage and there were floral borders and expensive-looking shops. Yet in neither town is there justification for such a gluttony of tinted shop windows and expensive goods, and both centres have an overwhelmingly unambitious and hopeless population. The only ones in both towns able to afford to drink are those still at school, and like their counterparts in other small towns the fifth- and sixth-formers in Southport were making their 53-pence half-pints of bitter last all evening.

Another remarkable thing all these small towns had in common was the evening dress code. On visiting Southport I was wearing trainers for about the first time in my life, because the sole of one of my leather shoes was in need of repair, and I'd just joined a gym. As Sod's Law would have it, most places in the one street with deceptively half-decent-looking bars had a 'no trainers after 8 p.m.' policy. 'Sorry, lads – no trainers,' we were told in about four places. Yet in every other respect we were clad like royalty compared to the Oxfam-shoppers of Southport.

Outside the pseudo-affluent acre or so of Southport there were no more theme bars, as presumably nobody could afford to do them up. We found a street with three adjacent bars, including one named Amsterdam Bar. As we approached it, a scantily clad woman with lots of hair and a face like a death mask flicked open the lace curtains and stared at us. However, the door was locked, and it had a discreet doorbell alongside it.

We decided Bar Amsterdam had better be on the list of those we missed out. Instead we crossed the road to a lively-looking bar which was playing inoffensive music, where we bought two half-pints for 53p each.

The barmaid and her friends there had a mixture of things to say about Southport. For some reason they wouldn't condemn it, yet they confirmed everything I'd seen about it. 'Hotels mostly *are* boarded up,' said one girl, 'but there are about a dozen nightclubs.' I asked where the sea was, for it had certainly not been visible from what Southport described as its seafront. 'It's no more than a mile from the Promenade,' she insisted. 'On a clear day you can see it.'

We discovered that particular pub was open until 2 a.m., so we left for a bit of variety. By this time the Amsterdam Bar had opened, and curiosity drew us in. It was in fact not a brothel – not as far as we could tell, anyway – but a transvestite bar. The blonde-haired woman we'd seen through the lace curtain spoke like Steve Coogan's Pauline Calf but with a deeper voice, which took us aback when she asked what she could get us lads to drink. The feminine façade only lifted away a few minutes later when her boyfriend came in and she got an erection beneath her tight black skirt. Still, hormone treatment had given her a decent pair of tits. We managed only the first half of our drinks before leaving, utterly miserable, for another bar. Both Simon and I realised this really was as good as Southport was going to get, and both of us felt a tidal sense of depression. Odd, given the distance we were from the sea.

Back out on the main street, which was deserted, as we could only have expected mid-evening on a Thursday, we passed a couple of places with names like Knightsbridge Restaurant. That place epitomised the pretentiousness of Southport, although as far as we could see it was the only restaurant in the town not spelt 'ristorante' – and that included the English ones.

Outside the town hall was a noticeboard displaying news of forthcoming local entertainment in the town centre. Mike Donahue and Ken Dodd featured prominently.

We turned left and saw another theme bar, described on the

outside as an Irish cocktail bar. What's an Irish cocktail, I wondered. A story about an Irishman's knob? I felt like going inside and announcing, à la Alan Partridge, that 'der's more to Oireland dan diss'. But Oi didn't. And in case anyone thinks I'm attacking Ireland, I believe a weekend in Dublin beats any that can be experienced in England, and it's where I proposed to my wife. (She said yes, obviously.)

Fed up with not getting into any bar because of my trainers, we made our way into the next bar by pretending to be surveyors. This was after a passer-by had advised us, 'You won't get in with those, mate.' The notebook and pen and my examination of the structure as I approached the entrance was enough to cause the bouncer to think twice about sending us away. But by that time we were on our third pint. All the bouncers we saw looked like ex-bus drivers. That particular place was called Baron's Bar – presumably in Southport that's how they think 'barren' is spelt.

Our next stop was a theme bar for the under-20s which had karaoke tunes being sung worse than badly to a loud and unmelodic 1990s noise which resembled the sound of roadworks. The beer was so universally bad in Southport that we couldn't face another pint. We agonised over whether to drink spirits or wine, knowing that we could have got bladdered on half-pints all night for less than the cost of a bottle of wine, but decided on splashing out £9 for a bottle of house red. It tasted as though it had been marinating a brothel's carpet for six months before being wrung out and bottled. It was Della Casa Rosso, bottled by S.p.A – La Mora – Italia, and distributed in the UK by Mondial Wine, London. You have been warned.

The youths in the bar were unapproachable and stand-offish. The decor was sparse and the place had been decorated in pastel colours, as happened a lot in the late 1980s before everyone discovered they had actually to pay for it all. We went upstairs on the direction of the DJ, who suggested we'd find a seat there. We couldn't – just a large space with young, awkward-looking poseurs standing and trying to look unconcerned by their lack of friends. The only memorable fashion statement was the girls' knickers – they all wore tight white skirts through which the floral patterns of their undergarments could clearly be seen. And they all stood looking as though they knew they had to be there but lacking the understanding as to quite why. The result was something that resembled a queue for the school headmistress's office, and the effect on us was to enhance our deepening sense of depression.

The young drinkers in that bar came in two categories: those who bought half-pints for themselves and made them last all evening, and those who bought bottles of Hooch and carried them from the bar, looking like milk ladies. Perhaps at one time they had worked for the dairy and were used to carrying bottles around in large quantities. It must have been Giro day.

Although the place itself made us feel almost suicidal, there was nobody we encountered who was particularly intimidating. The only intimidating thing there was the horrible wine. And the place turned out to be a nightclub. It seemed strange, since it was busy and at its peak at 9 p.m. I couldn't even explain this away by the fact that the following day was a schoolday, as this was August.

In desperation we went down to the ground floor, which, from the landing of the first, seemed to have less-inhibited drinkers. Sadly, as we reached there, the karaoke began again. Those singing to everything from house music to Burp, or whatever the Beatle-impersonating band is called, shouted into the microphone with not a care for the actual notes hit by the original singer. None of those in the bar seemed to care, let alone wince. This lot, I thought, is the budding new Hitler youth, and wouldn't recognise a discordant note if it danced on a harpsichord and sang 'discordant notes are here to stay', to steal a chunk of a *Blackadder* quote. Leaving three-quarters of the bottle of Château Sock 1998, we headed back into the night.

Even though it was only 10 p.m., we headed silently in the direction of the hotel despite the fact that we knew there were no pubs in its vicinity. In the circumstances, for once I didn't regret having left undrunk wine.

It was when we were just a few hundred yards from the hotel that we passed the Conservative Club. I beckoned Simon back and tried to convince him that we should enter for a laugh. He peered in through the door, through which could be heard the sound of an old piano playing wartime pub music.

I challenged him by saying that we'd never get in, so, treating this as a dare, he ventured inside. There was a sign saying 'All visiters must report to reception', which we did. Simon flashed his Lloyd's of London membership card, with me behind him flashing my press card, and we were invited to sign in as guests. Simon put his name down as Huw Jardon.

While the Embassy Club for the over-60s played on in the hall at the back, with old men in their yellowing pants and their younger wives waltzing across the dance floor, the front bar of the building had an off-the-peg collection of Tories. Don't get me wrong – I would never associate myself with Club Tories. Never again, anyway.

At the far end of the bar there was a group of men in their eighties in green sweaters and matching ties sitting on armchairs and drinking spirits. These people were the ones whose sprightly offspring were out the back dancing the night away.

At the tables nearest the bar was a group of three women, a middle-aged woman with a look that said she took life very seriously and two Southport peroxide blondes in their early forties. With them were a couple more people so inconsequential I couldn't even describe them. Suffice to say, like the rest of them, their idea of a good night out was to sit in the Conservative Club working hard not to buy a round. Of half-pints.

Simon and I greeted them and sat down with our pints. I struck up a conversation with the older woman and explained I was writing a travel book and was studying Southport. She told me she was the head of the Hoteliers' Association, before starting to rant like a politician about how much investment had been put into Southport, including a sea defence wall – the one whose casualty had been the sea. Then, getting into her stride, she said, 'This brought £7 million of investment to

Pleasureland, a multi-million-pound leisure centre, a lot of SRL capital, Lottery money won for the pier, a grant for the rest of the sea wall . . .' She was off.

I interrupted her to ask if this investment would provide a lifeline for the decaying and boarded-up hotels of Southport. This stopped her in her tracks. 'What did you say?'

I repeated the question.

She looked at me quizzically as though I was a complete idiot, and said with quizzical, Thatcheresque amazement, 'There *are* no boarded-up hotels in Southport. Whatever gives you that idea?'

I spluttered into my drink but answered the question: 'There are boarded-up hotels all over the place.'

'*Where* exactly? There are none – well, there is one right down there, but it's the only one,' she said, gesturing in the direction of the northern end of the Promenade. There was no getting through to her. Here was the head of an association who seemed unable to accept the rotten and decaying state of the properties of most of its members, the hoteliers themselves. 'Southport's hotels are in a good state of repair,' she insisted. I wondered by whose standards.

I showed her the postcard of our hotel with the address and phone number on the back, pointing out that the picture was of a building in good repair and must have been taken 40 years ago, since it didn't illustrate the potholes on the driveway or the litter on the lawns and showed a house whose exterior walls were considerably more than 50 per cent covered in paint. Her response was to argue that the new owners were not members of the association.

She began to look alarmed that I had formed what she saw (and wanted me to see) as a jaundiced view of the place. I reassured her I wasn't looking for reasons to be particularly nice about any of the places I was visiting. Then, because I had already accumulated various press cuttings on the book from people who had been expressing outrage at my remarks, I showed her the *Braintree Evening Gazette* whose front-page headline read 'UGLIEST PEOPLE IN ENGLAND'. Her face was a picture as she read more. Her expression was one of horror and disbelief – much as mine had been when she had insisted there were no boarded-up hotels in Southport.

The knives were out. She passed the cuttings on to her peroxide acquaintances, who read them and tittered, and she insisted I should not misquote her. Misquoting her I am not.

The husband of one of the blondes then came in, proudly carrying a miniature trophy he had won in a billiards tournament, and the ritual of who wasn't buying a round began again, so Simon stepped in and bought drinks for four of them. Then he asked the husband what he did for a living.

'I'm a grave digger.'

Simon asked him if he liked Southport.

'I do – there are plenty of old people, and I'm self-employed, so I'm never short of business.'

And battle commenced. Simon began. 'Of course, when they cremate people they burn two or three people at a time.'

The bloke slammed his drink on the table and furiously rebuked Simon. '*Nobody ever* burns more than one body at a time. You don't know what you are talking about. If anyone did that they'd be put in jail.'

Simon disagreed for the sake of a reaction. 'They burn as many as they can at one time,' he said.

The bloke was shouting by this stage. 'There is only room for one coffin. You are so ignorant!'

'No, they tip the bodies out and reuse the coffins,' said Simon, getting into his stride.

By this time his interlocutor was being warned by all his friends not to be wound up. 'You're so ignorant – you're asking for a fight.'

Simon rose to his feet and suggested they go outside. The bloke took off his glasses, jumped to his feet and screwed up his face as he accepted the offer. It took four Conservatives to restrain him. One of them, who had the stature of a Russian doll, warned Simon that if this guy hit him, his lights would go out forever. We were told to leave. I was more than happy to do so and left, cowardly praising the guy for his work, his correct views and his billiards trophy and apologising profusely for Simon, who, I explained, had had a lot to drink.

Tempting fate in a very real sense, Simon pointed at the psycho's trophy and said, 'Pocket billiards.' Fortunately this went over the guy's head.

'We invited you in as guests, and you've abused our hospitality,' one of them said angrily to me as we left. I thought that was rich – we'd simply come in and bought them all a drink. The fact that one of them was a psychopath who couldn't take a bit of ribbing without resorting to murder was hardly our fault. Simon's last words as we left were, 'He's pleased when people die, so he's mastered the art of killing.'

We headed off into the night, cheered so much by that little political incorrectness at the Conservative Club that we returned to the bar which we recalled was open till 2 a.m., where we met a bunch of girls who wanted to know more about the book. I went to the loo, and in my absence Simon told them I was a Tory MP. One of them, a 21-year-old called Louise, had fierce views on Southport: 'Every hotel is closed down and boarded up or turned into flats.' I rest my case. She said she was a counsellor, presumably for some busy local charity, and missed the irony when I said I was an MP. 'I know, Simon told us,' she said blankly.

At 2.30 a.m., after failing to find anything to eat on the way back, we reached the hotel to discover that the security code for the door lock had been changed. Clearly the work of the Hoteliers' Association woman, we thought. There was therefore nothing to do but sleep in the car. But as the psychotic grave digger from the Conservative Club knew where we were staying, we decided it best to drive elsewhere, lest we get beaten up in our sleep. So we drove off and parked in a layby not far from the motorway, to awaken three hours later and head for home.

In case anyone thinks I have been too cruel to Southport, here are some quotes from a website entitled 'The Real Guide to Southport', listed under 'Bad things about Southport' (http://www.elbowz.dircon.co.uk/southport.html):

Pleasureland. This has to be the most decrepit, dirty, funless funfair known to modern man. It boasts the world's oldest wooden roller coaster, which at least has historic interest on its side; elsewhere it's just a story of decay and neglect. It's probably the only site in the UK which would benefit from being turned into a retail park with a multi-screen cinema (notwithstanding the immediate death of the existing cinema which would follow) and bowling alley.

The oil rig (as well as Sellafield and God knows how many years of industrial pollution, mostly from Liverpool down the coast) has led to the water on this stretch of British coastline being amongst the dirtiest in Europe. (Good thing the sea doesn't come in very often, then.)

Old people. All over the place. Not just old people but bitter old people who object to you being young and enjoying the good time that probably passed them by.

The pier. Or rather the sorry disgrace that masquerades as a pier. The council needs a good kick up the arse and to make up its mind whether to either rebuild it or pull it down.

Sad twats who take their very shabby Escorts and Astras down to McDonald's Drive-Thru around midnight . . . these boys would like to be Max Power kids, but they can't even manage that.

The Orange Parade. A chance for a bunch of mindless bigots, and sadly some of their brainwashed children, to parade through the town, get drunk and fight. Unfortunately this happens every year, so Southport is best avoided around the weekend of Orange Day.

One final thing about Southport. Why *is* the local paper called the *Southport Visiter*? Don't they know how to spell visitor, or is it some evil plot to mess with our minds? I think we should be told . . .

3. Woking

Built to service the Brookwood cemetery

No study of British low life would be complete without a visit to Woking, home to Goldsworth Park, which is proudly proclaimed – rightly or wrongly – by its residents to have once been 'the largest housing estate in Europe' (their words).

Mysteriously favoured by Americans these days as a location for English country retreats, Woking has a history which is most appropriate to the modern town: it was built to service the massive industry down the road in Brookwood, a 400-acre cemetery. And the whole place has a moribund feel to it. Knaphill on the north edge of Goldsworth Park heightens Woking's attraction to death by claiming to contain the country's first crematorium. For a more diverse religious flavour, Woking is home to the country's first mosque, Shah Jehan Mosque, built in 1899. Woking is also the home of Britain's first Muslim burial ground, which was built on Horsell Common in 1917.

The Woking website describes the town as follows:

> Situated in north-west Surrey, 25 miles from London. Woking was originally a village located at what is now known as Old Woking, the current town centre being open heathland. With the arrival of the Basingstoke Canal and then the railway in 1838, Woking suddenly became more accessible from London and, in the 1800's (*sic*), the present town started to develop when London had a shortage of land.

What it means is a shortage of land *to bury people*.

The neighbouring village of Brookwood was also once home

to a mental home, set in expansive grounds, but it closed down and its inmates were released to the surrounding community. There is little to tell them apart. Now the site itself has been turned into a massive housing estate. How very Woking.

Goldsworth Park housing estate was built from the mid-1970s onwards on the western fringes of Woking on the site of what had previously been nursery gardens. It is still being extended 25 years later, and dwarfs what remains of the surrounding country. The colossal site has many tens of thousands of houses erected at the expense of a frightening number of trees – even more than the total number felled during the 1987 hurricane.

Woking itself is situated in the midst of Business Park County – or Surrey, as it used to be known – and is joined to each surrounding town by a mass of networked newly metalled roads and dual carriageways interlinked by roundabouts with peak-time traffic lights. Despite the thousands of acres of tarmac spilled over the countryside, there is still what locals deem to be 'an appalling road infrastructure'. However, plans for the creation of further road surface, in the form of a Woking bypass, have long been shelved.

There has in fact never been anything going for Woking. This was confirmed for me by a local cab driver, who proudly explained that the town's library has the honour of having been the first in the country to take the route of abandoning books in the early 1980s in preference for multi-media, long before the Internet was available for practical use to the general public.

Also among its claims to originality are its bars, which were among the first to adopt bouncers on their doors during weekend sessions. And among its claims to fame, as if the above were not enough, is the fact that one of the first inmates of the prison built 30 years ago in nearby Bisley, home of the National Rifle Association, was one of the Kray twins' hitmen.

Ask anyone living in Woking for a sentence summing up their views, and nine times out of ten you hear: 'It's a dump.' The ninth in my case was a lady taxi driver who started ranting on about how the owners of properties on the new estates get first refusal on local secondary school places, of which she said there was a great shortage. This presumably reflects a case of yet another local council being in league with building consortia and giving the new houses' residents first pick of the schools. I wait for the day when all local councillors are rounded up and shot.

Occasionally some of the town's residents will try and talk up its purpose as a town by describing it as part of the 'stockbroker belt'. I'd simply like to know why any stockbroker worth his salt would want to live in *Woking*.

Others illustrate that they feel embarrassed being asked about it. 'I *like* Woking.'

'Do you go to the pubs or nightclubs there?'

'No, I'm too old.'

'Did you ever do so?'

'God, no! It's hideous. It's just . . . *there.*'

'It's good for trains to London,' piped up another. So there's an easy escape route.

But mostly its inhabitants just display quiet resignation that they must live there.

Woking had one of the highest levels of borrowing per capita in the country prior to the 1987 crash (or so they say). Estate agents at the time took pride of place in the town centre, talking up the alleged value of two- and three-bedroomed terraced houses on the Goldsworth Park estate, houses whose interior walls were often constructed seemingly with just one sheet of plywood. Nowhere was the exaggerated escalation of house prices more tedious than in and around Woking, seemingly home to more staff employed in airport security than in any other industrial sector.

But it doesn't stop at the town itself. Residents from the surrounding municipalities have inflated airs about themselves, imagining some long-gone superiority about Surrey itself. Tradesmen such as gardening-tool vendors and estate agents adopt jacket-and-necktie attire when they frequent the bars in the surrounding one-time villages to assert their importance and to get slowly pissed. They achieve the same bizarre ritualistic

sense of achievement as bikers, considering first-name recogni-
tion a symbol of their status. Having been set such an example,
the road cleaners and unemployable of the villages do their best
to emulate this attire. Badly. Their undisguisable tattoos give it
away for a start.

Meanwhile the townsfolk worship the concrete South Bank-
styled arts centre, erected in Woking's town centre, which
houses a theatre. All well and good, except that its developers
then had to go and name it after a cross between a theme bar
and a budget clothes store – the Peacocks. Or at least that's how
it's known locally. To be more precise, it's called the Peacock
Centre, and it supports the usual provincial shopping mall, a
hangout for the town's uncouth young.

In the Royal Oak, an old red-brick pub in Knaphill, a
middle-aged local drinker took issue with my claims to be
meeting people in pubs to get a feel for the place. 'You don't
meet anyone in the pubs these days because they're all eating
places now.' And, sure enough, in Surrey there do seem to be
remarkably few plain pubs whose management hasn't been
taken over by some catering firm or other.

I felt short-changed when I went to catch my train back to
London at 10.30 p.m. I'd not really witnessed anything of the
people other than their reluctance to admit they lived there. I'd
heard it was a violent town, but had seen no real evidence.

The Woking ticket office was closed and the machine would
not accept my £20 note. So I crossed the road to the closing
Victoria Wine, acquired change and turned out of the shop
again to see two youths armed with a baseball bat indulging in
a seemingly unprovoked attack, beating the crap out of a
stranger. I crossed the road, the two lads scarpered and I bought
my ticket as the bruised and bleeding victim was attended to by
an unsurprised station guard. My education in Woking was
complete.

4. Slough

There are some places which have always been dreadful.
Slough is one of them

The deterioration of much of England has occurred only since the cultural revolution of the 1960s. Most towns only suffered the loss of their appeal when tasteless building work and over-population became rampant. But there are some places which have always been dreadful. Slough, like Woking, is one of them.

The reason for a dedicated branch line from Slough to nearby Windsor is said to be the fact that Queen Victoria couldn't stand having to step out from her train into Slough itself to travel by road the rest of the way. I can well believe it. Others claim it was Prince Albert who gave the go-ahead in 1839, presumably for much the same reason.

It's not easy to put your finger on exactly what is wrong with Slough. The name is a common Saxon word meaning 'mire'. Competing with Keats' 'And no birds sing' as the most depressing phrase in the English language is that which one hears as the train draws into the station: 'Slough, this is Slough'.

Forget John Betjeman, the first line of whose famous poem 'Slough' – Come friendly bombs, and fall on Slough! – is often quoted when the name of that town is mentioned (and sadly the US Air Force didn't miss Kosovo by *that* much). Just try waking up there in the late morning on a warm day with a hangover with the windows open. Add an easterly breeze, and the combined scent of curry and Mars bars is likely to trigger a physical and messy reaction to your alcohol poisoning.

While the smell of curry is not usually unattractive itself, coming as it does from the dwellings of the local prosperous Indian population, and while the existence of a large confectionery factory a mile or two down the road is not itself

usually a particularly nauseous feature of the town, it's what makes up the rest of the town that is so dank and unpleasant.

Slough is situated in what is referred to in the Home Counties as Silicon Valley. It is home to an ever-growing number of famous brand-name computer companies. But even prosperity of this nature has done nothing to add any kind of virtue to the town. Despite being located at a commuter-belt distance from London, it is by and large ignored by those who work in the City. In fact, those who work there tend to commute from London if they aren't already living in one of the surrounding towns such as Maidenhead.

Until the nineteenth century Slough was a quaint, ancient hamlet in rural south Buckinghamshire. It is hard to believe when visiting Slough today that the rougher residential districts of the modern town, such as Chalvey, were neighbouring villages until a few generations ago. Now it is an area better known for its trading estates than its Norman church and timber-framed manor house.

The arrival of the Great Western Railway put paid to Slough's role as a thoroughfare on the Bath Road, and given Queen Victoria's reaction a few years later, the creation of a hideous blot on the landscape was brisk.

Archaeology around the borough has thrown up signs of Mesolithic man. Archaeologists have pondered why, although Neolithic man built settlements nearby, no trace of them has been found in the borough itself. Maybe they had more taste than many do today. Even the Romans avoided it, stopping eight miles down the road at Maidenhead.

Why did Slough come into being if it was so awful? No one seems to be able to put their finger on it but the best guess is that the twelfth-century road to Reading and Bristol, known today as the A4, needed some kind of service station. This was not long after William the Conqueror had built the rather splendid Windsor Castle – the Middle Ages' equivalent of Chessington World of Adventures – two miles down the road. What was that about progress?

Judith Hunter does quite a good job in her book *The Story of*

Slough. It's a serious read, which is a shame because I thought from its title that I was going to have a laugh. I suppose I chuckled a bit when I discovered that the book, 'Town History No.7', has 11 full pages of adverts for things like 'Slough – Home of ICI Paints Division Dulux'. And 'Flexello Castors (Sales) Ltd'.

Hunter describes the difficulty historians have had mapping out an accurate description of Slough's past. One of the reasons is that there are relatively few records of the place, which I believe reflects a shortage of scribes. If that's true then it's certainly reflected in the modern Slough, where there is little call for anything in the way of a traditional library. Its local college, Thames Valley University – until recently Slough College of Higher Education – has in recent years been branded 'Britain's worst university' by the press. No small achievement.

In the 1950s, Slough's one remaining picturesque building, Hay Mill, which dated from the thirteenth century, was demolished by far-sighted town planners to make way for car parks and further trading stores.

It is not uncommon to read in the local (and national) press of savage murders committed by gangs in the town where, for instance, the victim's severed head is left by the roadside in one of the town's residential districts. A fair amount of fighting occurs in the town between different racial groups, often between black and Asian or between different Asian groups. The younger Asian generation, not just in Slough but in much of the country, is said to lack the respect and civility upheld by its elders at that age, possibly because they have undergone just that bit too much prejudice from the Anglo-Saxons. They have even developed their own variant of Estuary English. It includes the word 'innit' to replace, obviously, 'isn't it?' but also any other inverted verb formation, such as 'She's a tart, innit?'. But then you've probably seen *Goodness Gracious Me*.

Although the town overall consists of a major and industrious trading estate, those who live in Slough itself seem unlikely to prosper from it. Even the surrounding areas, places such as nearby Cippenham, spawn illiterate adults the height of whose ambition is to work in a hair salon. It does have the advantage to those who must pass through it *en route* to, say, Maidenhead that they can be assured of green lights at each junction provided they travel at 30mph, removing the need for them to pause in the place.

The local college itself is a national disgrace, with about the country's lowest academic standards and passes for anyone who bothers to enrol. I shouldn't complain. I went there for two years, spent most of the time in the bar and left with a merit-graded HND. I topped up my grant by copying on my Amstrad computer any work I had bothered to do, altering the layout and putting at the top the name of whoever was paying me a fiver to do so. A fellow student who never even bothered to return for her final year rang me soon after I'd completed my course to say she had received a certificate from the college which gave her a pass.

Essentially, like so many other grim and depressing places around Britain which have less than nothing of which to be proud, Slough is sepulchral, but it is also about the only place which at least does not appear to adopt that inappropriate sense of local pride I encountered in so many other towns.

5. Haverhill

A tidal wave of unmarried mothers

Suffolk gets a better press than Essex but parts of it make Braintree look almost civilised by comparison. Haverhill is a place where even the residents do not know how to pronounce the name of their town. Approaching Haverhill through gentle countryside had reminded me of *Salad Days*, but the only people I was to meet in the town itself were vegetables.

Passing from Essex into Suffolk you notice a massive amount of evidence of intensive farming. Surprised at the level of low life I was to encounter during my stay in Suffolk compared to that in Essex, which I had hitherto imagined to be the pits, I put it down to genetic modification of the county's residents themselves.

Of course there are some lovely and relatively unspoiled villages surrounding the Suffolk towns, such as Steeple Bumpstead, but on rounding a bend after passing through that particular village I was confronted with the sight of houses that had been spewed out over the surrounding hillsides clearly without the use of any town planner. These houses had a variety of views; chiefly these were oil works, reprocessing plants, factories, chimney stacks and pylons. This was Haverhill.

Attempts had been made at some stage to plant trees to conceal some of this from the road, but it had not worked. The trees themselves were struggling to survive or had died before reaching full height.

I entered Haverhill itself. All along the high street were boarded-up houses and shops. Every few hundred yards there would be a house which either wasn't for sale or did not have a satellite dish prominently displayed. I looked long and hard at the streets in the centre of the town but couldn't find a single house which lacked both features.

The signposts were twisted, giving me an eerie sense such as one would feel visiting Nagasaki or Chernobyl. In the town centre was a bleak Dickensian town hall with a satellite dish – or was it a wok? I wandered through and came out at the other end of the car park, where there was a sign trying to bring life to a place reminiscent of post-war Kosovo: 'Have a safe journey and thank you for using this car park.'

I turned a corner and saw a shop called Family Butcher, right next door to one named Pet Shop. That made me take a closer look at some of the townsfolk on the high street, many of whom were truly Braintree-esque.

Passing on through the town I saw some hideous architecture, and for the first time since visiting Hamburg in 1979 I saw houses the backs of which actually looked better than the fronts, with much of their hoarding vandalised.

A sign read 'Restricted access to town centre'. It was unclear whether this meant to cars or to pedestrians.

Haverhill is said to have more car parks per capita than anywhere else in the country, which is very odd since there is no reason why anyone should want to park there unless they were planning an insurance claim. There is truly sod all happening in the town. The only activity is shops closing down, while the only business activity is the recycling of 'Closing Down' signs. Those shops that *are* still open have signs pleading 'Everything at half price'. But at least the amusement arcade seemed to be doing a brisk trade.

The town appeared to have an inordinately large number of estate agents for such a small place. I counted six within a couple of hundred yards of each other, with little evidence of SOLD signs on any of their property adverts – presumably because *everyone* there needs to escape. The only other places open apart from the charity shops seemed to be these estate agents. I was taken aback by the prices. A property that would set you back by £30,000 in Derby would be over five times that price in Haverhill. Why? Christ only knows. I can only assume that houses are put on the market and just stay there as nobody in their right mind is going to pay £150,000 for a three-bedroomed house located in the centre of a stinking shithole like Haverhill. And, my God, does it stink. An inefficient sewage system combined in the heady summer air with the wafting smells from the nearby reprocessing plant, causing bile to dance at the back of my throat.

I only had to walk a couple of hundred yards from Haverhill's trading centre to reach the poor part of the town. Here people were truly creative as well as industrious. Not only had somebody stolen a red telephone kiosk whose red paint had all but peeled off, but he or she had wedged it in the front garden of a condemned but occupied terraced house between a birdcage and no fewer than three supermarket trolleys. To the front of the call box on its side lay a wheelchair.

In fact there were a lot of wheelchairs in Haverhill. A frightening-looking middle-aged woman with sideburns, walking alongside an elderly companion who was propelling herself along in a wheelchair, made me jump when her two-year-old daughter stood up in her pushchair to press the button on a pedestrian crossing. 'SIT DOWN!' the mother yelled, startling passing motorists on the busy A-road.

Back on the high street, as I walked through the pedestrianised heart of the town, battling against a tidal current of 16-year-old unmarried mothers, I passed a burger stand with a queue of at least 20 people. To the left was a shop with local announcements and classified advertisements. Displayed prominently among these was a Pest Control Service, specialising in cockroaches, rats, mice and rabbits. To my right was a pristine litter bin which could probably be sold on to another council with the description 'used only once'. Locals clearly preferred to walk among their waste than to section it off and, as they would see it, waste it.

I turned and saw a child in a twin pushchair drop her dummy on the paved road surface. It landed among dried dog shit, cigarette ends and the stains of drunks' vomit. The young mother picked it up and put it straight back in her daughter's mouth.

It suddenly hit me that there didn't appear to be any *single* pushchairs, and usually the people in the town were walking around as part of a family unit. With that reasoning in mind, I calculated that the average number of children per family in Haverhill was at least four. And the fathers all seemed to have their hair dyed peroxide blond in instalments.

On the approach to the arts centre, which was located in a converted church, I saw what I had long been wishing to see on this jaunt: a burnt-out Robin Reliant. I could almost have gone home there and then. But then I remembered I was still 55,000 words short of my publisher's target.

A moment later one pregnant teenager waved and yelled in some strange country tongue across the high street to another pregnant teenager. I am sorry I cannot tell you what she said.

A little further on I reached the first pub. It resembled those ones purpose-built in the 1960s to service council estates, even though this one was in fact on the high street. Up some brick steps was a patio in front of the actual premises where children could presumably drink, since the pub itself claimed on a sign on the door that it would not allow them inside. However, one glance at the floor told me why no parent should bring their children here: weeds, cigarette ends, dog shit and broken glass concealed the surface of the tarmac beneath them. Cleaning was not this pub's speciality. And all the benches had been vandalised. I gave it a miss.

Instead I crossed the road to a Greene King pub which on the outside advertised the sale of bar food on banners with two-foot-high letters. Inside I was told food was off. It was 1.30 p.m. I asked for a pint of beer. Beer was off too. I looked around at the decorations. The flowers were beautiful, but dead. And the cigarette machine had a security bar across it, such as I had only previously seen in Braintree. Behind it was the television. It appeared to have been bolted down.

Opposite the pub was a restaurant with a sign which made me chuckle but wonder if I was just being a snob: 'Good Friends Chinese and English Food to Take Away'. Walking through the entrance of said establishment was a man wearing a knitted jumper even John Craven wouldn't be seen dead in.

So I left to buy the local paper. Thirty pence entitled me to a copy of the *Suffolk Free Press*. Seven out of ten stories were about speeding drivers, two-thirds of the remainder about vehicle theft. The courts seemed to be very lenient in this district to the most jail-ready individuals who, once convicted, were given a conditional discharge, 'a drink problem and a miserable life' usually cited by the judge in question as reason enough for a non-custodial sentence.

The headline that day in one local paper read 'Expansion of camera scheme'. Its competitor, the *Haverhill Echo*, screamed 'Extra CCTV camera needed'. All very Braintree. An adjacent story was about an outbreak in the town of thefts of bicycles from back gardens. It made me again miss London, where at least I didn't have a back garden. On the next page was a story about Suffolk County Council awarding itself a 300 per cent pay rise, and opposite that was a page of barely coherent readers' letters, one of which quite reasonably asked how they could award themselves a pay rise when councillors were not supposed to be paid except in expenses.

I was still standing on the street when something caught my eye. Walking past me were two shabbily dressed people (which isn't saying much in Haverhill) wearing shoes from four different pairs.

A few yards further down the road was the Haverhill Job Centre. This was a hive of activity. It had a large floor space but all of it was taken up. There were at least four assistants answering enquiries, and in front of each of these was a queue of a further half-dozen. Curiosity drew me inside.

Behind those queuing for assistance was a car park-like maze of pushchairs, and behind these on the walls were the job cards, divided into various categories, the largest of which advertised armed forces overseas jobs – an escape route presumably for the young fathers who find they have over-populated their various families a little too early on in their career.

Two boards along to the right of this I saw no fewer than six women, children in their arms, crowding around a board which advertised building jobs. I couldn't establish whether these were for themselves or for their idle boyfriends who were in bed, in the pub or couldn't read. It might, of course, have actually been that they were looking for themselves: they would only be entitled to Job Seekers' Allowance if they actually looked for jobs, regardless of the unsuitability of the job in question.

Outside the building a few yards away was an approaching motorised street sweeper, unable to collect rubbish quite as quickly as it was being deposited on the streets. I wandered out of the town centre and on to a massive stretch of two-storey pebbledashed council houses. Every hundred or so yards was a green plastic skip. They didn't have wheelie bins in Haverhill, I concluded, they had wheelie skips. The surrounding streets all looked like Britain when it was run by the unions in the 1970s and when the garbage collectors seemed to be permanently on strike.

The Haverhill council had kindly saved ratepayers' money and planted fast-growing weeds rather than trees to conceal the abject ugliness of the buildings. A little further on I was quite taken aback on seeing someone in the town tending his garden. I turned back to take a closer look and felt at ease again: it was just someone stealing a neighbour's plants.

Round the corner was Boundary Road, which led to an industrial estate. Ahead of me was a massive, half-constructed and abandoned industrial complex with no roof. It and its surroundings had been fenced off and a 'For Sale' sign had been erected. Round yet another corner I saw the cleanest part of the town, something of which I could be proud: Murphy's petrol station forecourt. But this was the north end of the town and the stench of raw sewage was too much for me. So I wandered back into town, past a bollard which had been knocked over at a junction. The temporary surrounds placed there by the council to protect passing vehicles had been knocked over too and abandoned.

I walked on, past Station Road. Haverhill doesn't *have* a train station, so I assumed it referred to the police station. I kept walking, past half-painted houses, street signs covered by shopping bags and rubbish flying through the air. It really was diabolical. Opposite were rotten, corrugated allotments resembling a rubbish dump.

Then I reached the posh end of town, and I was back where I started: these homes backed on to the industrial estate. I came to a roundabout where the signpost pointed to the right to 'Cambridge and other industrial estates'. From there I made my way back into town and on to the tourist office to get a flavour of what might be considered an attraction in the area. The office itself was not much larger than the desk at which the officer sat. He was brutally frank when I innocently asked what attractions there might be in the area: 'I wouldn't say tourists come to this part of the world. You're better off going to Cambridge or deepest Suffolk.'

This particular trip brought me many surprises, and perhaps one of the biggest was that it was in Haverhill that for the first time in about ten years I came across a library whose primary purpose was actually to stock and lend *books*. There was shelf upon shelf of audio and video cassettes too, but these were not as prominent as the books. It made me reflect on the objective of *this* book: I was being less unkind to England than whoever it is goes around destroying it.

What's On in Haverhill was predictably short on detail. A one-sheet page, it informed me that special events that particular month were a Big Top Hip Hop and an under-13s disco. Also the Haverhill Sinfonia was performing Vivaldi's *Four Seasons*. I thought Classic FM had bought the recording rights to that – it's all they ever seem to play apart from Albinoni's Adagio and Pachelbel's Canon.

Bang in the heart of Haverhill is an attractive old church, through whose churchyard I walked. Its stained-glass windows were all blocked up with steel mesh grilles, the front door was chained and padlocked and the vestry door had been recently bricked up. So I gave up and left. As I did so, I read the sign out on the street which read 'St Mary's Church', specialising in 'baptisms and weddings'. Presumably in that order.

Haverhill was truly dire. It drove me to the brink of insanity, and I went into a high street broker's office out of sheer boredom to ask if they offered End of the World Insurance. It suddenly seemed apt. 'We can cover most things – I'll ask,' said the assistant. She returned with the manager, to whom I explained the reasoning. 'If Nostradamus is right then the world's going to end this August. But there are an awful lot of people in the world, not all of whom are necessarily going to die. What if you're only maimed? Can I get cover against such an eventuality?'

He nodded along with what I was saying, seeming to acknowledge the legitimacy of the risk. He said he couldn't offer it, being just a high street broker, but Lloyd's of London could. 'Just ring the switchboard and ask about a millennium specialist,' he said.

'You've been more than helpful,' I replied, and left with no such intention.

I returned to the pub with the dog shit and broken glass outside and ventured in to buy a pint. The place was packed with short, stocky, tattooed, unemployed thirty-something males with sleeveless T-shirts and cropped hair. They looked as if they were related but didn't know it. There were a few women in the bar too, all of them pregnant and all wearing creative maternity gear. The rest of the men's girlfriends were busy finding them work in the job centre.

I finished my pint and clearly it was time to go. After just half a mile I found myself out in lush countryside, albeit short of a few hedgerows, and the colour began to return to my cheeks.

6. Norwich

Genetically modified inhabitants

Norwich startled me at first, it seemed so civilised. The first day I spent wondering whether I'd wasted my time travelling all the way out to Norfolk to discover I was somewhere that wouldn't be appropriate to place in the same category as all the other godforsaken places I'd visited. I wondered if it would really be fair. But I persevered and, sure enough, by day two I had found ample justification for including the city. Not only is it situated right at the arse end of the country, but it truly is in decay.

For a start, it is located too far out of the way to be useful for anything to anyone other than the locals. A return ticket to London is 60 quid, for a start, and nearly two hours on the train.

I took a fast train calling only at Colchester (a dump I ruled out of my itinerary because I had met people from there whose only role in life could be to frighten children) and Ipswich (but not Bolton). After Ipswich the Norfolk countryside consisted of vast fields interspersed with vast reprocessing plants and farms. The traditional farmyard had now been replaced with rows of chemical storage towers. Here and there would be a bunch of bungalows dating from the 1970s.

The city of Norwich at first glance seems to have even more retardates than Wales. There are plenty with webbed feet, descendants from the Dark Ages Norfolk set who walked on stilts. Generations of ancestors have lived almost entirely on eels.

At first sight it also seems to give itself undue airs. But getting into the centre of the city, I realised this wasn't actually pretentiousness but a blend of old and new. If any place in the UK was to live up to the claims that most places make but patently fail to live up to, Norwich would be it. It left places like Gloucester far behind by claiming to be attractive and actually *being* so, not least by having ample mediaeval buildings still *standing*. Overall, the locals who expressed pride in their city actually had good reason to do so, I thought to my astonishment.

Not only that, but it had places called things like Bishopsgate which, unlike pretenders in towns such as Cheltenham, actually warranted their names. At last, here was a town which lived up to the description of being 'steeped in history', liberally applied without reason to places in virtually every other town I visited by bogus council tourism committees.

In Norwich the history really is everywhere you look. And unlike Gloucester its ancient buildings do not appear to be the central focus for the short attention span of local vandals who, I read that week, have finally managed to break away the last piece of Gloucester Cathedral that hadn't been protected with 20-foot-high fences topped with spikes.

But at the same time Norwich is heading for the inevitable meltdown that makes living there as dire as living virtually anywhere else in provincial England. On my second tour round the city centre, this time visiting the pubs, it became sadly apparent that the locals had a local council as obsessed with legislation as New World countries*. Which was ironic as Norwich is one of the oldest cities representative of the country

---

* The ACT legislative assembly in Canberra is running out of things to legislate on so has proposed to:
  - Ban transporting dogs on the back of open trucks unless secured by a short lead or in a cage
  - Have a curfew for cats where there is a threat to wildlife
  - Have dogs registered from 8 weeks old [previously 12 weeks]
  - Have dogs and cats compulsorily neutered unless owners have a breeding permit [for the animal, not the owner, I presume]
  - Only have one packet of each brand of cigarette on display in supermarkets etc.
  - Ban cigarette vending machines altogether in the ACT

which has the Magna Carta and which therefore doesn't need a constitution. But no, in Norwich, pubs all have large signs which read 'IT IS ILLEGAL TO DRINK OUTSIDE THIS PUB'. Suddenly I felt as though I was in America, at map grid reference N6 W45, where it would be ILLEGAL to, I don't know, fart in a restaurant, or N7 W45, to carry alcohol in your car. It was so paradoxical. Here was the city with the country's largest mediaeval city wall – built before the world leader in the random infringement of civil liberties, America, was even a foetus – doing precisely what it hadn't needed to do since it was first erected in mediaeval times. Norwich was banning things arbitrarily just because its current rulers, the Labour-dominated city council, didn't know any better. *Not* the way to run a successful society, and I thought the Yanks had proved that beyond question. Evidently not.

It had taken a day but now I could see just why my time was not being wasted.

In another Norwich pub, a local asked the barman whether he could leave his sports bag behind the bar while he did some shopping. 'Sorry, you can't, it's *the law*,' was the direct reply, delivered with no sense of irony. At first I thought this was someone trying to be mildly comical and referring to the tyranny of the landlord, but no: this was a local by-law. Suddenly Norwich really was Arse End territory.

I bought a drink and turned to a couple of retired blokes sitting at the bar. I explained what I was doing. Lord Melchett of Greenpeace lives in Norwich, so I thought it appropriate to use as an opening conversational gambit my view that in neighbouring Essex I'd seen examples not just of GM crops but of GM people. 'Some of the people here *should* be genetically modified,' replied the first retired gentleman. He paused, then added, 'In fact there should be a self-destruct mechanism for a lot of them.' He explained he had only moved to Norwich 18 years earlier, so was still most definitely classed as a foreigner. 'It's getting better, but I'm still foreign.' However, he did like the town itself. 'It used to have the best library I've ever seen, but it burnt down,' he said. His retired friend added, 'It wasn't arson, or at least they never proved that it was. I wouldn't be surprised if it was, the council in league with the building firm.' He was talking my language.

He continued, 'All the war records for the Norfolk airbase were lost. A new library is currently being built. Without a doubt it will be designed not to stock books. It's happening everywhere – a tremendous mistake in my view.' I could have stayed and listened to them all day but I had to go out and see more of the city myself.

I suppose Norwich really *is* the least objectionable place outside London. For the first time I was able to read a local newspaper which, while it tried its best to do a good job of painting a disturbing picture of crime in the town, clearly didn't have the fodder of local county courts brimming with car-theft defendants. And the place is not badly off – in the 1980s it was named Britain's most prosperous city. However, its principal trade is insurance. Need I say more? One hell of a lot of its inhabitants must be as boring as hell.

I started to retrace my steps and to seek out the tourist office. Norwich is not fond of maintaining signposts for pedestrians except on the actual street where the destination lies; for instance, on Station Road there's a signpost to the station, and on Castle Street there's a sign pointing up to the castle. But there's no telling unless you have a map that the tourist office is hidden at the far end of the market.

Inside the tourist centre, once I'd *found* it, I was amazed at the first experience I'd had of queuing at one of these places. This felt surreal and I wondered if I was really doing my job, visiting somewhere people actually seemed to want to visit. I ended up spending £5 on two small 30-page booklets on Norwich before wandering back out into the marketplace and down towards the pedestrianised centre. There was clearly a lot more wealth around Norwich, and after what had seemed like a year in Haverhill it suddenly felt great to be surrounded by people who for the most part used two legs standing up to get around rather than two large and two small wheels sitting down. Even the Oxfam store was clean, didn't smell musty and had newish items on sale.

All the bars in Norwich allowed children – perhaps because landlords had lost their right to run their establishments as they saw fit and now the local council had made it ILLEGAL for them to refuse admission to children. One pub I looked in with the idea of eating lunch resembled a school dinner hall with a scattering of teachers.

I went into a rough-looking empty pub in the centre of the pedestrianised district where loud music was blaring out of the speakers and where the barman had more tattoos than a Braintree mother. I was the only patron. 'Is it always this busy?' I asked. I shouldn't have done. I was about to escape when a possible transvestite minced in wearing lumpy skin-tight lycra trousers and pink hair in a ponytail. Limp-wristedly he/she ordered a half-pint of beer.

As he/she walked out of the door, the barman called out, 'Sorry, mate – if you drink, can you drink down there to the right? It's the law round here.'

I asked the barman what he meant and he explained that outside and to the right was a ghetto which the council had ringfenced for what he called 'the winos'. 'The council won't let us buy that plot of land. If we did we could evict the winos. Only trouble is, the council reckons they'll just move on somewhere else.'

'You get a lot of "winos" round here?' I asked.

'Thousands,' he replied. 'Every penny they get, they spend on booze.'

The place was now filling up. The barman was busy and the availability of vacant stools, all of which seemed to lean at strange angles, was diminishing. A huge woman came in, sat on a bar stool and it collapsed. I felt sorry for it. She brushed herself down and, seeming to be humiliated, left without buying a drink. 'I superglue 'em together each morning,' said the barman, a bit taken aback. 'Usually they lasts all day.'

Apart from being a little frightened, I was also getting peckish, so I wandered on a little way through the paved streets before finding a row of about four encouraging-looking restaurants all with a common Norwich theme: Tuesday to

Saturday lunchtime two-course special for a fiver. I sought the best menu and was about to walk in when I saw there were no ashtrays. I scented a local by-law to the effect that one was not allowed to smoke indoors. But no, provided I sat at the back of the restaurant out of view, they would bring me an ashtray.

The restaurant itself was a peculiar mixture of traditional and modern-style decoration. It seemed an oldish kind of place with a well-worn tiled wooden floor but with the same kind of abysmal music playing as everywhere else I'd been to in Norwich that day – the sort that in the early 1990s used to appeal to 14-year-old Americans whose turntables swung both ways. This kind of sound, one to which the sound of loud retching would have been preferable, seemed to dominate Norwich's cafés, restaurants and bars.

The girl serving me had pretty strong views about the city. 'The people are fairly friendly – that is, the foreigners are friendly. The Norwich born and bred are backward thinking. But enough people have moved to the place in the last few years to make their unfriendliness unnoticeable. In the 1980s Norwich was full of dog poo. Now it's full of foreigners.'

By foreigners, she explained, she meant people like herself. She came from Winchester. And she had the best description to apply to the 'great nightlife' in the city: 'It's very quiet,' she said. Then she lowered her voice. 'I can't really describe it as anything other than great. My partner organises it,' she said by way of explanation, confounding me further still. She must have noticed me looking perplexed, because after a pause she said excitedly, 'At 2.30 a.m. people are in the curry houses. At 4.30 the streets are filled with seagulls picking up the remainders of the takeaways.'

'Oh, *right*,' I said.

A group of blokes in a nearby pub all with a traditional Norfolk accent were of a different view when I asked what the local nightlife was like. 'Girls all want to get their tits out,' said one, to the philosophical nods of his friends. I moved slowly backwards then fled to another pub up a hill where I saw a Channel Four TV crew filming three blokes for a new chat show. When they'd finished their interview I asked the presenter, a shapely young black woman with as much air in her head as Vanessa Feltz, whether she had seen, heard or read anything about this travel book by Bill Murphy. As I got to about word four of the question her eyes began to lose their focus and her head to twist slightly to support the strained frown across her face. I paused and she looked blank, so I said, 'It's been in *The Sun* a couple of times. And *The Mirror* . . . describing locations around England and . . .' She cut me off. 'No, man, we're strictly LE.'

'What's LE?' I asked.

'Light entertainment,' she said, before turning and leaving the pub to escape any more difficult questions. As far as she was concerned, her job required her to be outgoing calls only.

The impression that Norwich is in its dying days as a pleasant town was forming rapidly. Such a tribute leaves it slightly out of step with the rest of the country, but according to the gits who run its council, it is 'the fastest-growing region in Britain'. So it doesn't really stand a chance. I give it two years tops before there ceases to be any attraction in getting on a train for two hours travelling north-east of London.

The University of East Anglia is another downside to the city of Norwich. UEA produces what it calls graduates in subjects like economics, yet these people clearly don't know the first thing about the function of an economy. Admittedly, it's not Slough University, but it could almost as well be.

I met one such graduate in a Norwich theme bar, who told me she was doing a degree in media studies. 'So, Athena, do you want to work in print or broadcast journalism?' I asked when she explained that she was in her final year.

'I'd like to work in TV . . . or ray-jo . . . no, TV.' She paused, thinking for a few seconds, before concluding, 'I like black eyeliner. Black kohl, from Boots.'

She would make a great weather girl.

Was this the best UEA could produce? I can only assume the dim Channel Four producer I'd met laying down the law on 'LE' had graduated from the same establishment.

7. Huntingdon

A people who aspire to the forces of mediocrity

Throughout my research for this book I kept encountering a sense that there do not exist in the country any elected local councillors who don't make a living from backhanders from building firms. I'd never been to Cambridgeshire before but was stunned by what I saw: mini post-'60s housing estates were scattered liberally around the edge of every town. Biggleswade was the most laughable, with hideous mock-Tudor 1990s erections randomly placed on the edge of town.

Huntingdon itself looks okay on first glance, but stay a little longer and you discover it is rotten to the core. The people of Huntingdon are the quietest lot in England. They sit in their quiet plush pubs discussing their mediocre lives working in the service industry. It's as if no one wants to raise their voice for fear of standing out, which suited me fine when I was there. Or at least that's mostly the case. Every few minutes you hear the sound of a car driven by the educationally subnormal broadcasting offensive, loud and hideously discordant sounds which pass for music among the under-18s these days.

The place is so quiet that the usual posture of bar staff is to be seated on the customer side of the bar staring into space with a cigarette. And two out of three people out during the day are over 60, for this is where Londoners like to come to retire. This passion for over-populating what once was Huntingdonshire is to blame for the new 'building programmes', according to one cab driver there. 'People from here can't afford the new prices. London's created its own market. It's great for me – they all want cabs. But what about the rest? Got nowhere to live.'

The thing about Huntingdon is that it is a nice place with a quaint town centre but with a people that aspire to the forces of

mediocrity. For instance, as soon as you arrive there by train you're given a taste: a sign dominates the car park indicating sponsorship by some power company or other, which clashes with what remains unspoilt in the sleepy town. Huntingdon is so quiet, nothing seems to be happening. Its population is unreactive. But I noticed too that there was not a smile on anyone's face all the time I was there. And that includes the tourists, of which there were plenty – although none of them were in the tourist office when I turned up there.

It was only after I had stood for ten minutes, while the sole assistant in the booth finished her phone conversation with her mum in which she described in detail her plans both for that night and for the night of 31 December, that a queue had begun to form behind me, and she finally said, 'I've got to go – I'm at work.'

I pointed out to her that all the guides on the shelves referred to a place called Huntingdonshire, which I thought had been abolished around a quarter of a century earlier and absorbed into Cambridgeshire. 'That's just poetic licence,' she said. 'Anyway, they're thinking of bringing Huntingdonshire back.' If that was so, I wondered, why does the council-sponsored, glossy, advert-ridden but *free* guide to 'Historic Huntingdonshire' refer to the offices of Huntingdonshire County Council, whose head office of the same name was based in, ur, Cambridgeshire? Seemed a curious way of rigging things.

I was not surprised but nonetheless a little dismayed when I turned to page one of the guide to find that top of the list of things to do in Huntingdon was 'shopping', with a boastful description of how the town was filled with exactly the same shops you'd find in Walsall or Wolverhampton or anywhere else in the bloody country. I was even more dismayed to find that Huntingdon-'shire' tourist office could not give me a directory of pubs in the area.

Historic Huntingdonshire is a thick publication with black-and-white outline maps of every town. And the maps are the greatest turn-on to a developer, providing as they do the potential for further building in a style which is in keeping with the rest of the towns, which are largely kaleidoscopic images of cul-de-sacs spreading in every direction outwards.

The *Huntingdon Town Crier* meanwhile is an amusing little rag. The front page was devoted that day to a story about John Major and George Bush. Page three had the regular car-boot-sale story located centre-page. Most of the rest of the paper was about thefts from caravans, money and jewellery thefts, drunken youths in a street fight in a nearby town, a Huntingdon man using his grandmother's house for his drug-dealing caught speed driving in St Ives, a young woman assaulted on a Huntingdon bus, the theft of a mountain bike and the theft of wrought iron gates, and there was also a story on how police are warning locals not to be victims of summer theft, of which there appeared to be no shortage. Oh, and the abandoning of guinea pigs on a doorstep. I jumped in a cab to take me to St Ives.

8. St Ives

*A perfect example of a local council's criminal
environmental damage*

Over the course of the eight-mile journey by cab between
Huntingdon and St Ives it was clear what had happened: the
patchwork quilt of meadows and fields of Cambridgeshire had
been replaced by a patchwork quilt of new estates. Every hectare
was now occupied by planners, builders or their dreadful
finished product.

The centre of the small town of St Ives is delightful providing
you are standing in one of a few positions where there is no sign
of shopping chains, notably the ancient stone bridge which
crosses over the Great Ouse – a delightful experience on a warm
summer's day if you do not look far to your left or right.

It was on the bridge that I was due to meet a camera crew
from Anglia TV which was doing a feature for its news bulletin
on tourism in the region. The presenter was an attractive blonde
whom I first bumped into as she politely noted down the names
of local retardates who were asking for a signed picture which
she would post on to them. I introduced myself and was given
a despairing look at first until they realised I was actually one of
their official interviewees that day.

I had arrived a little early. I was asked what I thought of the
area, and whether I'd put it in the same category as, say, Woking
or Slough. I began immediately to spout off about the place,
about the overcrowding of the countryside with new estates,
generally condemning the area. 'This is all good stuff,' the
interviewer said, 'only can I ask you when on air not to use bad
language?'

I think I'd used the word 'arse'.

'I won't do so on air, I promise,' I said. Then I noticed

71

another interviewer was licking the arse of a Huntingdon local councillor, so I added that the people at fault for the destruction of the country were just that type of people. 'Show me a non-corrupt local council and I'll show you little green men on Mars,' I said – or words to that effect.

'You *can't* say that on television!'

'Why not?' I asked. 'It's fair comment.'

'Well, there are legal implications.' Anglia TV's 6 p.m. news bulletin was clearly not a news programme which involved any journalistic investigation, but simply a magazine programme. They told me to come back half an hour later for the live filming. I sauntered off to a nearby pub.

I'd taken the first sip of my pint when I was rung on the mobile with some unlikely-sounding story about the satellite being down and having to pre-record the interview. So I left it and returned back up the road. There they sat me down beside the river and spent no more than 30 seconds filming me state my views on how the place was not really what it claimed to be for tourists, for obvious reasons.

'Great – thank you for not swearing. You can go now.'

I was a bit miffed.

'This will definitely be broadcast on the six o'clock news,' the interviewer said. The six o'clock news on Anglia TV is clearly, to use TV parlance, 'strictly LE'.

Indeed, the programme was broadcast in said bulletin. Among a collection of the usual MPs and councillors was the owner of a local Aston Martin garage in Newport Pagnell, a town I didn't even visit. On being told my views he said, 'Rubbish! Absolute rubbish! There's plenty of good things about this area. It's close to the M1, and you've got Milton Keynes just up the road.' I kid you not. (Milton Keynes, by the way, cannot be classed as 'decaying'; it never really *was* anything to start with.)

A history of the district explains how every couple of hundred years buildings of previous eras were knocked down to build shops or accommodation for a population which was rising to replace the one which had been as good as wiped out by the plague. So it can be argued that there's nothing new in what's happening in terms of population shift and building. But for the first time, huge swathes of the countryside are being destroyed forever by the building of bogus homes.

Every young person I spoke to there looked and sounded bored out of his or her tiny mind. In the hideous-looking bar beside the Bridge, I asked the barmaid what she thought of the place. 'I'd like to live somewhere else. There is nothing to do here. There are just three nightclubs for the whole area,' she said. Bar work was not what she had planned as a career, but what can you expect when you go for a degree in art and design? Unlike most 'graduates' in that subject, she was at least working for a living.

St Ives is just a small place with a large surrounding population. I shall not be returning. I don't need to travel all the way to north Hertfordshire to find Boots, Woolworths and other such stores.

9. Barging through the Midlands

*I wondered what was concealed
beneath the grimy surface*

Train journeys were driving me round the twist, so when in the midst of my travels I received a call inviting me to join some friends on a canal barge I leapt at the opportunity. For a start it meant I wouldn't have to set foot in either Birmingham or Coventry yet I could still include them in the book. Personally, I think the Luftwaffe could have done us all a favour and finished the job in the case of the latter. But then, to be fair, I could say that of a lot of English towns.

There was nothing worth speaking of during the first half of the canal journey. Birmingham looked slightly cleaner than it had done the last time I'd seen it ten years earlier, but it was only new brickwork that I could see from the canal, not the shit it concealed.

Countryside became more open as we left the centre of the industrial Midlands and moved along to places like Polesworth, where we disembarked for lunch. There I learnt from the landlady and a supportive local that things had improved greatly in the area. The occupants of the housing estates were much less trouble than they had been in recent years, they assured me. 'We used to have bouncers on the pub doors Friday and Saturday nights, but we don't need them no more,' said the local with a strong Brummie accent. But I was getting used to this by now: most canal cruisers were from the industrial Midlands. It takes that particularly dour personality to invest in the same kind of holiday that you take year in, year out, where all you're going to do is steer a long barge along a narrow water-filled carving through the industrial countryside, greeting all and sundry with no respect for how lousy they might be feeling in the damp, overcast weather.

The longer I spent on the boat, the more annoyed I became by the ridiculously friendly nature of everyone we passed. While there was no apparent legislation against being drunk in charge of a barge, I could almost sense a system of penalties being handed out to anyone who failed to greet passers-by, whether they were on the towpath or in passing boats. It's interesting to note that 'tow' is spelt how a Brummie would pronounce it.

One bloke in the pub in the village of Polesworth, a few miles west of Rugby, insisted there was nothing grim about the area and gave an annoyingly long list of sites tourists would find interesting, notably Roman ruins, Roman forts and the site of the Battle of Bosworth Field – which I always thought was in Leicestershire.

'I'm more interested in what these towns are like to inhabit at the close of the twentieth century,' I said, and as I did so I wondered how long it had been since I'd heard it called that without the use of the m-word. But he wasn't listening.

'Robert Peel was born in Tamworth, three and a half miles away. Tamworth Castle – now there's a place worth visiting. Norman, I think.'

I tried again. 'And new developments? Like the local crime rate?'

He sort of understood. 'Tamworth – only real-snow ski slopes in Europe. And only 16 miles to the Birmingham Mezzanine. Tamworth's a bit hectic,' he added, catching up with my question. 'There were problems, but people mature as they grow up. Lot of bloody smashing 19- and 20-year-olds round here now, cosmopolitan ages – they mix with the 60-year-olds.'

So I turned to the landlady and asked if she experienced trouble in the evenings. 'No, we ask 'em to leave if they're any trouble, and call the police if they don't,' she said. 'You get a few weirdoes, going round drinking other people's drinks.'

I tried not to laugh.

The bloke was determined to make his pride in the place known. When I asked him if he could justify the local inhumanity of local man to local man – nicking each other's drinks – he argued with a shrug, 'Everywhere's like that now though, isn't it?' It seemed impolite to disagree, even though it's not a characteristic I'd come across in bars in the past.

The countryside between Rugby and Polesworth and beyond is littered untidily with caravans and inhabited barges, so I asked them in the pub whether they experienced much trouble with travellers. 'They're New Age travellers, and the new-age New Age tidy up after themselves,' explained the landlady. 'You used to see piles of rubbish. Nowadays they bring empty bin bags and leave with them filled.' Perhaps they really *were* a more civilised bunch than those in the south.

It was summer, so a large proportion of the barges were occupied by holidaymakers. All of them addressed each other in very familiar tones. At one point, as we parked up ahead of a series of locks, the guy in the barge ahead of us presumed we were staying and began addressing no one in particular in our party: 'D'yow now where to gow?' He kept repeating this, before saying, 'It's ownly £1.14 a pint owver there.' After a few minutes, with no progress having been made in the queue for the locks, we decided to heed his advice just to get away from him. When we returned an hour later he was just moving off. 'Sow yow took me advice – £1.14 a pint owver there.' His vehicle drifted off at the regulation 4mph and we never saw him again.

There is in fact more countryside visible from canal level in the Midlands than you'd imagine. I wondered what was concealed beneath the grimy surface – vehicles, prams, fuel tanks and tons and tons of litter, presumably. Where we had been moored, the side of the bank indicated to us that there had recently been a serious flood, for it was strewn with all kinds of litter.

Later that day we stopped at the first of a series of towns I had never heard of and which I am sure I never will again. These were backwater places with nothing particular in their favour and which were as populated as the average small English town but very much sleepier and immeasurably less unpleasant to visit. I feel I would be doing an injustice to them if I were to name them, as that guy did a few years ago to the south of

France in his books on Provence. At least I am happy to say that when we went for an Indian meal in one such town the food was appalling, with the greeny-white sauce accompanying the popadums as far above room temperature as the rest of the sauces. Given that many people before me had dipped their popadums into the same dish, I imagined it to be teeming with bacteria and gave it a miss.

The next stage of our cruise took us through the heart of Nuneaton, past dank-looking canal-side streets with such dining establishments as the unfortunately named Wing Fat Cantonese restaurant. As we progressed to the east of the town the canal began to be lined with new houses. Not hundreds, but thousands. On our left they all looked the same and had 20-foot gardens, and on our right they were more robustly built and had 200-foot gardens. Most of the latter had garden gnomes or mock Greek statues on pseudo jetties where they met the canal. The purpose, as far as I could see, was to make out that they were 'posh' to any curious passing Midlands boater.

The boat took a sharpish turn to the right, and as it did so the horizon opened up to reveal countless thousands more houses and housing developments on both sides of the canal. All of them looked as if they had been built in the last two years – that is, those that weren't still in the process of being built. They stood in clusters, some of them a hideous collection of new, oddly coloured and uniformly ugly houses planted within a mess of cul-de-sacs, all with the same make of satellite dish and burglar alarm. Without the latter, the contents of these buildings were presumably uninsurable.

All of a sudden we were treated to variety: the left side of the canal continued to bring us more and yet more houses erected in the last few years, while the right seemed to be the *Guinness Book of Records*' entry for the longest uninterrupted stretch of allotments. About 100 yards behind them was the most frighteningly long row of new housing developments.

If so many hundreds of thousands of new buildings have been erected in the past decade, why do those currently residing in Downing Street insist on a need for so many more to be built in the lifetime of the next parliament? Is it to secure an election fighting fund? It means that wherever you are in the Midlands you are never far from an army of builders. Christ knows what would happen to the unemployment figures if some government administration were to put a stop to house-building licences, although I suppose these people could then get jobs in the demolition trade. It's equally frightening, of course, to imagine how whatever currently remains of the countryside will be killed in a very few years if they *don't* stop building.

A little further south of Nuneaton, electricity pylons decorated the landscape, with housing estate after housing estate nestling in clusters at their feet. From there, for the next few hours we were never out of earshot of a motorway or major highway. Also, as it was the school holidays, we were treated to the constant sound of 'Greensleeves' emitted from ice-cream vans which seemed to be following our route.

In spite of the surrounding ugliness, canal wildlife seemed to be flourishing, including the most amazingly patterned dragonflies which frighten the shit out of people when they cross between the banks, missing their faces by about an inch as if through a sense of malice. They frightened the shit out of *me*, anyway. Nature seems to be restricted in the Midlands to these narrow stretches of waterways, peaceful now but for the quiet rumble of the engine and the periodic hiss of electricity pylons.

Suddenly we were confronted by a barge containing the kind of people who actually *live* on these boats. Moored up alongside a car breaker's yard, the barge which caught our attention had boarded-up windows and at the front stood two fat, scruffy, unclean, unshaven, middle-aged blokes. At their feet were three children of between four and seven years, all with weathered complexions, playing with dirt. I assume the people who live in these abodes can seldom afford the fuel to move on. They'd presumably stopped there to siphon petrol from the car wrecks.

Beyond the scrapyard, a litter-strewn playing field was surrounded by a group of large, grey municipal buildings and a reprocessing plant. Between there and the horizon were estates of new buildings. Between us and them, something that looked like a dead otter lay face down in the canal. Dead was the only kind of fish visible in that stretch of water, while dead hedgehogs floated between the litter-infested reeds. The canal was built over 220 years ago but now it is struggling to cope with the level of toxic shit man is depositing in it. I lost count of the number of polystyrene fast-food boxes floating on the edge of the water in that section of the journey. It was an inhospitable and hopeless wilderness, with even the donkeys who stood in the occasional field looking ill-treated and sounding vexed.

Our driver, Mark, was the subject of abusive threats concerning his steering. Fortunately for me I was not on the steering committee, seated as I was safely at the other end of the barge. 'You're revving too much!' was a common refrain from vexed barge captains passing the other way as our barge veered towards theirs in the current. Across the water, more land was congested with mechanical diggers preparing the foundations for yet more houses.

At Hartsbury Junction we had to turn off to the left to join the Oxford Canal, so we stopped for a spot of lunch. We entered the Greyhound, an obvious calling point for boaters following our route. It was five minutes past two. We asked the landlord for a menu. 'Try our dining-room,' he said, miserably.

'What about these blackboards?' Mark asked.

'They're pub snacks,' the landlord replied. Mark shrugged and asked the rest of us from the boat what we would like to drink. Two of us asked for pints, which Mark ordered before turning to ask the other three. One of the girls paused. Just a few seconds had passed since the pints had been ordered, but the unpleasant git behind the bar, sounding like a member of the Gestapo, ordered, 'Hurry up! Come on – I haven't got all day!'

Five minutes later, after we had seated ourselves around a big table, Mark returned to the bar. 'We'd like to order food,' he said politely.

'Only doing sandwiches now. Everything's turned off in the kitchen. Sent the staff home, too,' said the landlord. Fine, so we ordered sandwiches. Funny how at 2.05 p.m. the dining-room had been at our disposal but come 2.10 p.m. there was nothing left to cook.

At 2.25 p.m. three lads asked at the bar for a round of drinks. 'It's past time – can't you see? Gone 2.30 p.m.,' they were told gruffly.

'This *is* England, isn't it?' they asked loudly – and to my approval – as they left. A series of other holidaymakers came in to meet with the same warm reception. So Mark went up as well just for the hell of it. He got the landlord's wife, who addressed everyone as 'loov', or 'loovs' if there was more than one of them. 'Pint of Pedigree, please,' said Mark. She dutifully pulled a glass from the shelf above her but caught the eye of her husband, who shouted across to her, 'Do you know what time it is?' She shrank away.

The Greyhound was a tied pub which served a good pint of Marston's, but I wondered what chance the guy running it was giving it of making any money. Why do people enter the service industry in the first place if service itself is such an alien concept to them? But then I wondered if it was just that the Midlands is such a miserable area that people like this consider it their duty to reassert that particular feature.

We left. Ahead and to our right we could see the M6 tearing up what remained of the countryside as we passed through Ansy and noticed its Social Working Man's Club selling beer for a quid a pint.

That afternoon, like much of any canal trip, was uneventful, if not a little dull. There weren't even many locks to pass through to alleviate the tedium. Come the evening we found a couple of adjacent pubs at Newbold-on-Avon and sampled both of them. In the second one there was a 25-year-old karaoke singer belting out songs much older than she was, while I was disturbed to see four children in one corner of the bar, sitting from the time we arrived until our departure at around midnight, paying full attention to nothing but the singer herself. What was so disturbing was that these children ranged in age from about four to about nine years, yet they were silent bar the occasional mouthing of words to familiar songs. The four-year-old boy sat cross-legged on the floor beside the table singing along to 'Saving All my Love for You', while what looked like his elder sister sat on the bench gazing at the dance floor. Every few seconds the whites of her eyes would show as her eyeballs disappeared from view. It didn't bear contemplating what life experience she had endured to mute her so much, or even wondering what regime caused them all to sit in silence, at the height of their childhood, in a crowded bar until gone closing time. Every now and then two smiling drunk women would come over with a soft drink for them and sit with them for a minute or two, before returning to the raucous adult male company they were keeping at the other end of the bar.

As time wore on the pub filled to capacity, mostly with women, who were all dressed in clothes you'd have expected them to have been wearing a decade earlier. They were all either very thin or very fat. I overheard one female Laurel and Hardy duo discussing the lacy underwear they had seen earlier that evening in nearby Rugby train station's ladies' loo, and how it made the place look like a prostitutes' changing-room. I'm sure it did, loovs. It was all too much for me, and I staggered back along the canal to collapse into our barge.

My last impressions of the district were formed on the final day of the trip when we paid a visit to a canalside pub which advertised itself as being the last for five miles. At the back of the pub was a theatre kitted out with lights and a small stage which we could see through a locked window. The act itself I heard each time I visited the loo – and you know how it is, once you've had one piss you subconsciously feel you have to keep going for more with every subsequent drink. As I passed the doorway to the stage I heard loud but third-rate singing and acting, and rather hoped none of the packed-in audience had had to pay for the experience.

As I took my seat back in the bar, I saw at the next table a boy of around seven or eight drop his drink. He began to cry and his father sent him round the table to his mother, where, instead of being told he was a clumsy young git who should be more careful, he was picked up and cuddled. His sulking behaviour had been a devious way of getting at his sister, for whatever reason, a conclusion I drew from the malicious face he pulled as his back was turned to both of his parents. I despaired: the molly-coddling continued and the boy turned out to be a complete wimp. But so were his bearded New Age parents. At school – if, indeed, this was the type of establishment he ever attended – he would clearly get beaten up every day with increasing force. What sense of justice were these people teaching their child? That nothing is ever his fault? That he'll get a hug every time he is upset? Because the real world's just like that, isn't it, girls and boys?

As if that was not enough, through the window I saw another child of a similar age acting up, presumably in despair at the poor acting taking place on the stage. And instead of getting a slap, he was picked up by his father, who walked him a few times around the courtyard telling him everything was all right before returning to take his seat.

A few hours later our barge reached a town with a train station. I made my excuses and caught a train back to London.

10. Brighton

If you ever want an excuse for not paying taxes, come to the Costa del Dole, or Brighton

The 10.08 to Brighton took me south from Victoria through the grey, endlessly run-down, graffiti- and estate-ridden ghastliness that is south London. There were around 4,000 square miles of grime and crime between the train and the horizon. I've known a handful of people in my years living in the capital who swear by south London. All I can bring myself to do is swear *at* it. Why anyone would want to live there is beyond me. Civilisation doesn't begin until you're north of the river and in what London Transport refers to as Zone 1. Ask a black cab to drive across any bridge after 6 p.m. and he'll almost always turn his head away and drive away rapidly. Especially if your address is Deptford, Purley, Croydon or Thornton Heath. You might just as well live on Exmoor.

The only visible houses for ten miles as you head out of Victoria are dilapidated terraces. Okay, there are a few more trees per acre, but they simply make good hiding places for muggers.

The train sped on through Surrey, a county which doesn't seem to *have* countryside in the traditional sense. Instead it has become a network of large building estates with a few pre-fab fields scattered in between. About the last of its trees fell over during the course of the 1987 hurricane. Yet the people of Surrey try and perpetuate a sense of being *in* the countryside, with a significant number of them wearing brand new Barbours and carrying walking sticks. I shut my eyes and didn't open them again until reaching my destination.

Some 40 hours later I wished I'd kept them closed. If you ever want an excuse for not paying taxes, come to the Costa del

Dole, or Brighton. The town is full of individuals who all look the same, the vast majority indulging in the 'Who can have the most body piercings?' competition. Most of them look like rejects from the *Dr Who* props cupboard and beg the question – did they get the piercings to impress their friends or to ensure they'd never get a job? Both, probably.

Brighton's claim to fame is that it has the largest homeless population in England, with a huge number of heroin dealers and certainly the highest number of drug-related deaths per capita in any English town. My first impression of the place was the sight of two designer-label-clad *Big Issue* salesmen at the station's exit both trying to fund their heroin addiction. One was on his mobile phone, dealing. The other was well dressed and clean shaven but had a nasty sneer for anyone who declined his offer of a paper.

I picked up a copy of the local paper, the *Evening Argus*. It seemed my job had already been done for me, with countless letters inside regarding the departure of Lord Bassam, leader of the local Brighton and Hove council. This man appeared single-handedly over 12 years to have engineered the creation of a blot on this coastal landscape to compete readily with England's other scum blackspots, and the local people's protestations make my analyses of other English towns appear positively optimistic.

Locals express views such as 'The town is full of drunks, beggars and dead-end kids, making Brighton a no-go area for most decent citizens' and claim 'The filth, degradation, influx of deadbeats and complete ignoring of local feeling must be seen to be believed'.

I anticipated stumbling across the machine that churned out these beggars, junkies and drop-kicks who stand around on every corner, but that machine sadly is Brighton's own over-eagerness to embrace the politically correct madness and to over-extend the welcoming hand of social benefits to all and sundry. Let the fuck-ups of England unite. Come to Brighton! It is the beggar, junkie, alkie paradise of England! Let all our dreams die together in this innocent town.

So on to the statistics. Highest homeless population, worst

heroin problem, most deaths from AIDS. Perhaps Brighton is, unbeknown to its residents, the equivalent of Sellafield but with human garbage being dumped here rather than nuclear waste. Given the choice, I'd go for Sellafield; at least nuclear waste is invisible.

The other big news that week in the *Evening Argus* was of a drugs raid at a homeless centre. There was an immediately recognisable difference between the homeless of London and the homeless of Brighton: the latter clearly does not need to be homeless. Homelessness there is simply a fashion accessory.

The place is known for its white middle-class population and, to those who move here, as the home of a council which just gives away dole money. From the idle youths' perspective, if they are going to sit on their arses all day, they might as well do it by the sea.

I was interested to discover in talking to some of the unemployed Brighton citizens who *were* trying to find jobs – and, believe me, they were in a pitiful minority – that there is supposedly very little concern from employers with regard to replying to job applications. 'Half my dole money seems to go on stamps, and I *never* hear anything back,' said one design graduate. I'd have written him off as being unable to put together a convincing job application if it hadn't been for the fact I heard another group of people saying the same thing – probably the only other group of applicants in the area – and if I hadn't read a letter that day to the local paper from a vexed potential employee calling for legislation obliging employers to reply to applications. I didn't grimace; I accepted I was in the provinces.

Top of the list of places of interest in the town is the West Pier, an ugly monstrosity of rust supposedly set to be reopened. Looking at it, I thought the only people who'd want to venture on to it would be suicide cases.

I asked a middle-aged guy on his lunch break in a town-centre pub what he thought of the place. He was gainfully employed and I thought at least *he* might provide me with something against which to offset Brighton's ample selection of

bad points. 'It's full of pretentious no-hope dreamers. They are a lazy, cliquey bunch of cretins,' was his reply. I wondered whether I really needed to stay any longer. 'They must be putting Valium in the water supplies,' he added. His friend of around my age said he had lived in Brighton for ten years but had finally had enough. 'Everyone under 40 spends their life talking about how they're going to release a record or make a film. By contrast, in London their equivalents talk about the record they have just *released* or the film *now showing* in the West End.'

Fittingly, he added, the quality of the water on Brighton's beach is never believed to pass EC standards.

I walked down a narrow pedestrianised street known locally as *Big Issue* Street and thought that never have John Lydon's words 'There's no future in England's dreaming' been more true, at the end of the song he sang under the guise of Johnny Rotten, 'God Save the Queen'. Brighton is the sort of place where you'd expect to hear the sound of England grinding to a halt.

A few yards on, outside a vegetarian food store – of which there are many in Brighton – I saw two female beggars arguing. 'This is where *I* work,' said one, angrily. Brighton beggars belief, I thought.

I did meet *one* industrious and comparatively stable youth who had made capital out of making records. 'I live here because it's cheap,' he explained when I asked why he was still living in Brighton following his success. We got talking and he agreed it was the place to come for the dole. 'A friend of mine gets £76 a week with no need to sign on. He's depressed. Classed as sick! The pubs fill up with these people at lunchtime on a weekday.'

Living in Brighton with a full-time job, however, is anything but cheap. Rent increases have been accelerating in recent years at a rate far higher than in London, with a two-bedroomed flat often over £1,000 per month – or considerably more than the monthly cost of a mortgage on the same kind of property in London.

I could include here observations on the famous homosexual 'community' of Brighton, but firstly I would be jeopardising any profits from the Pink Pound, and secondly, to be honest with you, I didn't really see any. They keep themselves to themselves. They are said to take more in the way of drugs than any other group in Brighton – presumably because they've got more cash than the pure wasters. 'The gays in Brighton are on a non-stop party mission,' said one barman who asked not to be identified. He had a gay flatmate, he said. 'This afternoon he and some of his friends came back to the flat and tried to push a pill down my throat. They probably wanted me all loved up,' he told me.

His assistant behind the bar had previously lived in north London. He intervened in the conversation. 'The gay community only go to gay pubs. They drink in Camptown, sister district with [London's] Camden. They keep themselves to themselves.'

It seemed to me that in Brighton most of the people who were neither DJs nor drug-takers were in the local cemetery.

A notable feature of Brighton is the presence of the fag hag. These are gorgeous-looking girls who will only hang out with gay men in gay bars which play cheesy music because their first, disastrous, experiences were with local wide boys and consequently they now consider all men to be 'bastards'. Their understudies were to be seen all over the place in the company of skinhead Neanderthals.

What puzzled me was that the town does not really have that many jobs going anyway, so why should people head there claiming to look for work? Because they know they'll never find it? American Express, I discovered, is about the only major employer in the district.

I asked another guy whose name was Mick his views on the place, and felt even more satisfied my first impressions would prevail. 'It's cliquey. People who hang around in groups won't even acknowledge people who pass them even if they've met them a dozen times before if they don't fit into their clique and dress the same.' Obviously that's not many.

He continued, 'The type who move to Brighton are alternatives who are too lazy to make it in the real world. They reject society but the truth is that society rejects them. Having lots of slash marks on their wrists symbolises to them that they've made it in life.' So, a modern equivalent of the Duke of Edinburgh award badge, then.

He kindly took me to another pub to see what he called 'the crusties' but was disappointed when we got there. The place was empty. 'It'll be because of the wet weather. They only bother to get out of bed when it's sunny,' he said. We left, passing a 16-year-old girl who stuck her tongue out to nobody in particular for the sole purpose of displaying the studs she had in her tongue. Mick continued, 'They all try to walk around like Cockneys, would-be Londoners,' as a heavily pierced skateboarder free-wheeled past down the hill. If any of these people wanted to fly to another country – not that they would, as they'd sooner spend the fare on drugs – they wouldn't get through the metal detectors at airport security.

'Everyone in Brighton is an aspiring DJ. But Fat Boy Slim is the only one ever to have made money in Brighton,' Mick told me. I suddenly felt quite honoured at being one of the few non-DJs in the town. 'It's London by the sea. A handful of people make money out of music but out of all the years I've lived here I've only known one person achieve any success. Even Primal Scream left because there was no future here.' The band that was flavour of the month the week I was there was a female equivalent of the vulgar Geordie band The Macc Lads. 'You have to indulge in extreme eccentricity to make it above the rest,' he explained.

For the rest of them, life seemed to be one long excuse, a big wall of impossibility.

Physically Brighton is a disgrace. There are roadworks and building works in just about every street and, according to the locals, all the council does once it has narrowed one street is widen another, perpetuating the sense that it has no policy on roads at all. Others go further, saying the council has more money than sense and therefore it just erects buildings for the sake of it.

The town looks like the City of London soon after the 1993 IRA bomb, with scaffolding lining the front of most buildings.

'Last week I saw an old lady with a walking stick cut off in her path by new building works and no warning of them. I had to run across the road and stop her from being hit by an oncoming car,' said Mick's musician friend who had joined us. 'Still, all this scaffolding stops the burglars going hungry.' So there was at least one philosopher living in the town.

He said he thought the best thing about Brighton was the price charged for drugs. 'There are more drugs in Brighton than anywhere else in the country. They charge the best prices and you get the best deals here. I speak as someone who has taken everything under the sun,' he assured me.

A guy at the next table leaned over and volunteered his own summary of Brighton: 'Too many on the dole, too many wannabes, too many dreamers, too many cafés, too many alcoholics, and the traffic system is shit.' Well, I already knew that, I said. He persisted with his solution. 'We need to have trams here rather than cars in the city' – very new Labour. 'A lot of the accommodation is shit, and most of it is owned by one man. Too many students. High turnaround means everything is transitory and no repairs ever get done. The properties are just left to deteriorate,' he said. 'People are not homeless – there are too many soup kitchens and the dole office is too friendly for that to be the case.'

The letters page of the *Argus* is revealing too. Brighton, of course, encompasses the nearby municipality of Hove, a hove of activity for the retired folk of the area or for train-spotting thirty-something cycling fanatics. There, while there are fewer losers, there is every bit as great a sense of pollution as in Brighton, according to letters to the local paper. One reader described Hove's public lavatories: 'To say they were in a filthy state is putting it mildly.' The other letters complain about 'hooligan girls' on the buses, town facelifts which left 'flowers half-planted and left to die in the heat – a waste of money', and a scandalous residents' parking scheme which can only serve to line the council's pockets (how *very* unusual).

I walked from the town centre towards the coast. Amidst the drugged-out pubescent youngsters hanging out on the streets there are a few fish and chip shops where you can get cod and chips and change from three quid. Turn the corner at the seafront and suddenly the price rockets. Suddenly, even in the most insalubrious of cafés, you're in tourist rip-off territory – there are signs everywhere which read '£7.95 for two courses'. What these places fail to point out is that it's even more for one course, and suddenly that is the theme of the couple of acres or so of Tourist Brighton: outrageously priced food in themed streets for the non-discerning tourist.

I set off to find cheaper but less contaminated fish and chip shops but couldn't. Suddenly I was in vegetarian this, vegan that land, all at ridiculous prices. Beans and lentils were in. Meat was out – and, glancing at a few of those indulging in such malnutritious delights, so was a healthy complexion, though it was often difficult to tell beneath the bronze and aluminium decor they wore.

I ended up eating at Burger King and felt more than satisfied, before heading for a pub – any pub – passing on the way a crowd of well-kempt, expensively clad *gits* selling the *Big Issue*. Outside the Lamb and Flag, a run-down, odorous and condemned building by the square, was one such vendor in new-looking heavy brown velvet trousers with a new-looking bright red sweatshirt and expensive trainers. I couldn't resist replying to his '*Big Issue?*' with 'You really *look* homeless, don't you?'.

'What?'

'Well, you're hardly short of money, are you? You make me sick,' I said, getting a bit carried away as I walked into the pub. I don't think I should have said that because he reached for his mobile phone. A couple of minutes later I had bought a half-pint and turned to face the door, where I saw a group of young Chinese lads approaching him. As they got near I saw him pointing to me. I felt unwell. There were three of them, so they must have been Triads. I went to the toilets, where I removed my glasses and jacket before returning to take a different seat.

An hour and a half later I glanced outside. The aggressors seemed to have gone, and there was a crowd of malingering Spanish students indulging in their national pastime – kicking their heels – on their last night in the country. I slipped out and pegged it to the station.

11. Macclesfield

*Macclesfield man drinks until the
women become attractive*

Simon had another meeting to go to in the north-west so I thought I'd travel some of the way and take a look at Macclesfield. I'd never been, and knew nobody who actually came from there. However, a dozen or more people had told me they had at some time had the misfortune to work in or visit the place and they assured me it was dire.

In fact Macclesfield amazed me. A whole cluster of unusual things about the place makes you want to leave as soon as you set foot out of the station. The first is that no matter where you stand in the town centre you are in sight of a sign pointing to the Samaritans. The second is that just about everyone in Macclesfield is physically unattractive. And the third is that just about every shop is an estate agent. Look in the window of these and you're in for a shock: a two-bedroomed terraced house costs as much as it would in London. A large number of new three-bedroomed houses were on the market for £365,000. *Why?* Apart from the local petro-chemical industry, there's very little going on. Except for estate agency. And that's according to the local tourist office. A travel agent had a big poster offering four nights in Dunblane, which suggested a macabre side to the people of Macclesfield. And it was a good thing I hadn't planned spending the night there, for hotel accommodation is about as over-priced as the real estate itself.

It was still early and we wandered into the town, which is built entirely on a steep hill. So this must have been where they filmed the Hovis advert, I thought as I climbed a one-in-three cobbled street.

The ugliness of the people of Macclesfield was certainly

greater than that of the women in Braintree, where there are quite a few attractive young ladies, albeit pregnant. Women in Macclesfield, however, are redeemed by having at least some degree of personality. Many of them speak like Bubbles in *Absolutely Fabulous*, and the voice of a simpleton is always amusing. By contrast, there is nothing to laugh at in Braintree. The physical appearance of Macclesfield woman is remarkable. For a start they are all muscular, with large hands and arms. And there were absolutely none you could term attractive, at least not the day I was there.

Another difference between Macclesfield's ugly and those of Braintree is that I could see no unmarried women in Maccles-field, although to look at those wearing wedding rings it was hard to understand why anyone would actually want to *marry* any of them.

There is a distinct lack of coffee shops in Macclesfield, unlike towns in the south. Was this because it's cheaper to brew your own, I wondered, conscious of the innately frugal nature of northerners. I guessed the only place they relax is the Samaritans. We did find one café but it had closed down, presumably due to lack of business. It's a brave man who sets up a non-essential business in the north. According to the local tourist office, there are no fewer than 11 cafés and teashops in the town. Well, *we* couldn't find any of them.

I was stung for 30p when I bought a local newspaper, the *Congleton Chronicle*, incorporating the *Macclesfield Mercury*. Half the front page consisted of adverts, as did all of pages two and three. In fact there was considerably more advertising in this rag than you'd expect to find in the free trade press, which I'm told people only read for the adverts. It was impossible to find anything consequential in the paper on which to base my research, presumably because the place itself *is* so inconsequential.

In another newsagent's I found the *Macclesfield Express*. One story in there (unlike the *Chronicle*, this one *had* stories) described how nearby Poynton suffered on Friday nights from 'gangs' of 500-plus rampaging youths. Surely with numbers that vast, the word 'gang' wasn't quite the right choice.

The youth of Macclesfield all looked unemployed, and many of them unemployable. I was passed on the street by two techno-hippies in new designer-label patched flared jeans and T-shirts with Asian print on the front. There were other local fashion statements in the town: in every shop I entered, the staff were all wearing overalls, and half the women wore black bras beneath white blouses, creating a contrast with their red faces.

A notice outside the town hall registered the three candidates for the forthcoming election: a Liberal, a Conservative and an independent candidate. So, no one's wasting time or lost deposits fighting for the Labour party. Nicholas Winterton was Macclesfield's MP.

It was still only 10 a.m. and Simon and I both felt exceptionally depressed. 'Let's go to Crewe,' Simon said after we had drunk our coffee in McDonald's. Well, we tried to escape, but at the station it soon became abundantly clear that we would be waiting half the day for a train. So, foiled, we returned to the town. As we did so, we passed a NatWest bank with a poster reading 'You could be £20,000 better off with our big, big competition'. Beneath it someone had printed '(Lloyds, Barclays . . .)'. As we looked at it, we witnessed an irate manager tearing it down, angry at the actions of an irate customer.

We kicked our heels until 11 a.m., opening time. As I bought a round, I asked the guy serving me what he thought of Macclesfield. 'I've only been here three weeks, but they are a very odd lot. All of them – they drink very heavily.' It was as I suspected – the guys in Macclesfield drink until the women become attractive. It was cheap beer, so the local council was probably subsidising it for the sake of generating local heirs.

The light humour did not prevent us from feeling utterly depressed, heightened by the fact we were imprisoned by the local train services, predominantly Virgin. We trundled silently on to the White Lion, which for some unknown reason had a collection of Victorian irons on display, chained down. The number of prominent CCTV cameras on the streets suggested there was a great deal of crime in the town. The pub itself was like a time warp. We were the only people drinking there under

the age of about 60. We left half our pints and wandered towards the station, near which we found a bar. The people running the place looked miserable, presumably from a lack of custom, and the pub next door had given up the ghost altogether. They had electricians rewiring the place. One of them had jottings and hastily written phone numbers tattooed on his arms. I'd never before seen a tattoo reading 'Call Bob – 01543 . . .' but I surmised Bob lived in Staffordshire.

We sat in silence, watching the time creep slowly by. With half an hour to go before our train, we crossed the road to the station, where we stood on the platform and discussed Macclesfield. 'I take it you don't like Macclesfield,' said a woman sitting on a platform bench.

'Are you from Macclesfield?' I asked.

'No I am *not*,' she replied firmly. She began to tell us how miserable the place is but how she had to come here from Stoke to visit her mother in a home. 'There's only one train every two hours. If I ever meet that John Prescott . . . I'd like to ram his two Jags where the sun doesn't shine,' she said, before launching a further series of understandable tirades against Richard Branson and the social services who were making her mother's Alzheimer's disease that much more unbearable.

Let me elaborate on Virgin's services, at the risk of losing Virgin Publishing as a potential publisher. Much of my travel was done in hot weather, and on Virgin's trains as often as not the air conditioning didn't work, if it indeed existed. Whenever I have travelled Virgin Airlines with my wife, the seats have been noticeably more cramped than any other airline we have used. We travelled on one crowded Virgin flight to our wedding in Boston. On the return flight to England, my wife was told, seemingly arbitrarily, that her small backpack containing a few wedding gifts was too large to go on the plane and needed to go in the undercarriage. She pleaded with the guy that it contained breakable wedding gifts, but to no avail. Meanwhile, other economy-class passengers were passing on to the plane with two or more times as much hand baggage. When we finally got home we found that our Waterford

Crystal gifts that had been snatched and put in the hold were all smashed.

Anyway, the Virgin train finally arrived at Macclesfield and in the stifling heat I drifted into sleep. The last thing I remember before awakening five minutes short of Euston was being shown by Simon the moorland north of Stoke-on-Trent, where Donald Neilson tortured and dismembered his victims.

12. Romford

'More villainies than England ever knew'
- The Ballad of Captain Blood

Heaven help us all. The fact that Romford exists is enough to drive the most rational man to religion. The place is in your face from the moment you arrive till the moment you leave. The exit from the station into the town itself is partially blocked by a hoarding which reads 'Cheque's (*sic*) cashed instantly!'.

This was the first time I'd ever disembarked at Romford, although I'd been on many trains before which had stopped there. These included journeys to Gidea Park, where I'd sometimes end up at the end of a night, drunk and asleep and 20 miles beyond my intended destination of Stratford, where I once had the misfortune to live. 'Journey time back home from work' was one reason I'd left that area for the relative safety of Bethnal Green.

On days or nights when I was sober enough to see what was going on as I sat on trains stopping at Romford, I noticed one constant: the people who lived here were clearly poor in every respect, notably that of taste. I recalled this distinctly as I ventured bravely into the town.

Out on the street to my left was the town centre, so I strolled off to the right instead to see what lay outside the shopping malls. Not a lot was the answer. Wide streets suggested business had once been busy, but now the streets away from the town centre resembled those of a US ghost town. Victoria Street had on offer a pram shop; a closed motorbike shop; an Asian takeaway (closed); a pizza takeaway; a Cypriot restaurant due to reopen under new management in the coming weeks; a shoe repair store, with a sign saying it was moving premises; a vinyl LP store selling rap and garage music which was *open*; a derelict insurance broker; a closed designer clothes shop; an *open* hair stylist; a sewing centre; a security shop; two estate agents, both *open*; a closed chicken and rib takeaway; an *open* café; and a queueless Citizen's Advice Bureau. That took me by surprise, as insecurity about jobs, money, housing and relationships are at the root of most problems with which it has to deal. Romford looked like a place where everyone suffered from all of these, and more. I had no choice but to see the town centre itself.

Passing through the throngs of well-built men all wearing gold necklaces, I returned to the main street of the town, passing closed employment agencies and open bookmakers. The only really happening place in Romford seemed to be McDonald's, where I endured an extended queue for a snack as locals pursued their hobby of queue-jumping. They all looked a little too aggressive for me to try and stop them and so I waited patiently to be served a cheeseburger.

Thus fortified, I continued on to the centre, where I noticed a scarcity of signposts pointing to anything in the concrete, mugger-friendly shopping district of Romford. But signs of a different nature all over the place did catch my eye, such as the large sign which read 'WE DO NOSE-PIERCING HERE' in a jeweller's window. I wanted to find the local tourist office, and as these are usually located next door to town libraries, that's where I headed.

It was Thursday, by this time 11 a.m., and the Romford library was *closed*. Beside it, outside the town hall, was a noticeboard of expired notices from the London Borough of Havering. I saw a guy carrying a pile of books try the door. 'It's closed,' I said helpfully.

'Yeah – ridiculous really, isn't it?' he replied as he walked off.

But could I find a tourist office? Could I *arse*. So I returned to the town centre via the unemployed-friendly subway, where I saw my first signpost of the day. It pointed pedestrians in the direction of the DSS office.

It was time for a drink. I went into a large non-themed bar, where I ordered a half-pint of Tetley bitter. When the barmaid handed me the perfectly healthy-looking drink, she asked, ''As that got enough 'ead on it?' I said it had, thank you, at the same time wondering how long it was since anyone had ordered anything other than lager in a Romford pub. But then I tasted it and realised bitter was not the only ingredient.

A blackboard behind the bar displayed the current discounts, which included £1 for a bottle of Babycham. I hadn't seen or heard of Babycham since the 1970s, and yet here were chilled shelves stocked full of the stuff.

It wasn't yet noon, though, so the hardcore of Romford still hadn't come in for its hair of the dog. The only other drinker was an old geezer in pale blue shoes and a misshapen brown jacket and tie just sitting looking angrily at anyone who caught his gaze – in this instance myself and the three bar staff. After a while he got up and shuffled out, giving us all venomous and reproachful glances of hatred.

I left soon after, tiring as I was of the taste of pipe-cleaning fluid, and made my way through the maze of cheap clothes shops, Debenhams and discount stores. Two out of three stores had closing-down sales, and two-thirds of them actually had the word 'discount' in their original names. I reached a large, open, 1970s-style paved square bordered with shops, and as I did so the sound of what I thought had been a shop's stereo system became louder still and I realised there must be a 'busker' somewhere nearby, presumably wheelchair-bound, earning a living by illustrating the art of sitting alongside a battery-powered stereo amp-speaker system annoying the hell out of passers-by.

In fact it turned out to be a guy playing an electric violin to the backing sound of 'Don't Cry for Me Argentina'. And as soon as the track finished, it repeated itself. Over and over again. I wondered if he was busking but when I got closer I saw he had on sale for a fiver each a collection of CDs, or CD's as they're called in Romford. Some 48 hours later I still couldn't get that wretched tune out of my head.

To his right was a closed-down British Gas showroom, the end shop of a parade of yet more shops advertising the fact that they were closing down. I wondered if there were plans afoot to raze Romford to the ground and rebuild it. I asked the owner of a shop called Suit Clearance, who said there were no such plans. 'This is just a knockout shop – all these stores along here are. We're using it as premises to sell off last year's stock we bought on the cheap,' he told me. The shop was rented on a short-term lease, he said. 'It could close next month, Christmas, next year – we won't hear till it happens.'

In fact the whole of Romford appears to be a shop graveyard. Not only that, but the monstrous leisure centre across the road from the town hall has been closed down. The local *Romford Recorder*'s letters pages were filled with pitiful claims and counter-claims by competing councillors regarding its future. It is a fine example of what happens when resources are left in the hands of such people.

There is only one reason why a business folds, and that is bad management, according to those employed by the creditors, the receivers or the liquidators who have to come along, pick up the pieces and salvage whatever they can. If that is true then there cannot be a single living businessman in Romford. And Rom-fordonians, before you protest, drug-dealing *doesn't* count as a business.

With such a high turnover of shops in the district, it made sense that, when I looked around the local job centre, I could see an abundance of positions for shop fitters to add to the list of pub, catering, drivers and other universally manual jobs on offer.

Round the corner were yet more stores with 'MASSIVE DISCOUNTS' printed on their windows. Next door to a children's clothes store in its last days before relocation was a hair stylist's training centre. Hair is something people of Romford *do* spend money on. And still there was more to discover just in Romford's shopping district. Round yet another corner I reached Yates' Wine Lodge, one of around 30 that I would see in total during the eight months I spent researching this book. I peered in through the window and saw it was only occupied by the elderly. This was what happened in Romford: the 'theme' bars run on the theme of coffee mornings for the over-60s.

In a nearby newsagent's I bought two local papers with a £20 note. 'Ni'-ee' faw'een change,' said the spotty youth who served me. To perfect the Romford accent you must drop as many consonants as you can and leave a fair amount of guesswork without losing complete sense of what you mean.

Displayed on the wall of a nearby hardwood bar – don't ask me to name it because I can't remember – were the stories of three historic figures from Romford. One was a local knight who married the daughter of Henry de Montfort, godson of Henry III. The second was the Poisoner of Navarre, Henry IV's father-in-law, who was freed rather than executed in return for becoming an informer and who retired to Havering. The third was Captain Blood, who arrived in Romford in 1668 and had a fitting ballad written about him posthumously, containing the couplet:

> Here lies the man who boldly hath run through
> More villainies than England ever knew.

Funny that – it's villains who still seem to make up most of the modern population of Romford. It's amazing the groups of spotty youths who wander the town's streets with nothing to do with their time. By night these groups are the ones labelled 'gangs' by the local press. Essex-wide newspapers, fulfilling their obligation to write about Romford, only seem to find the column space to refer to criminal activities which occur in the place. Obviously I don't live there but I have no reason to think that there is anything else newsworthy about the place, although Hornchurch and other surrounding towns appear to suffer just as much. There the youths do things like dislocate 90-year-old women's fingers as they steal their pensions. The Romford 'gangs', meanwhile, like to leap out of cars and attack defenceless youths their own age on crowded streets, secure in the knowledge that nobody's going to stop them. There was an interesting report in the *Romford Recorder* the day I was there about an appeal for witnesses to the *woman* who seriously injured a *man* during an argument. Another one reported road rage against pensioners. And in Seven Kings, not far west of Romford, a detective constable was beaten up by youths when he tried to arrest them. What larks.

On Arcade Place, off the main street close to the centre of the town, is the Romford Snooker Club. I went to take a look. Its front window had been smashed and entry was via an answerphone system to members only, so I gave it a miss; I've seen *EastEnders*.

I stuck my head around the door of the Firkin pub, but the place reeked of cheap men's perfume so I gave that a miss too. Feeling generous, and completely out of character, I dropped a quid coin in the hat of a beggar who was accompanied by a dog wrapped in a blanket. What was his response? I'll tell you: nothing. Not a single bloody word of thanks. I was going to take it back but reminded myself that this was Romford and just walked on, thus freeing an extra column inch or two in the local press for letters from local councillors saying how attractive the county has been made thanks to their efforts. What a load of *bollocks*.

On I walked, past a sunbed centre advertising 'futuristic beauty' – an appropriate title, since beauty was certainly something that hadn't yet affected anyone in Romford.

I walked past a decaying Tudor-looking pub, the Golden Lion, occupied by some of the army of builders that live in the area. They were sitting, I noticed through the smudged windows, drinking cans of beer.

By this time I was carrying more souvenirs and newspapers than I could manage, so I queued in Millet's to ask for a carrier bag. The assistant who answered my request was wearing a badge which said 'Here to help!'. 'We're not allowed to sell carrier bags,' she said sternly when I said I was after one, as though it was a local by-law.

All day I had been looking for a bookshop in Romford. I had my suspicions confirmed in WHSmith, whose manager said it was the only bookshop in town. This didn't surprise me – it's not the sort of place where you envisage the residents ever entering a shop like Waterstone's. And the library was closed.

WHSmith didn't stock the book I was after, though the assistant offered to order me a copy. This was obviously no use to me, but she did at least give me a carrier bag.

It was lunchtime, so I went to grab a drink and a snack. I couldn't face Yates', but went down the road to a similarly themed pub and ordered a glass of wine. I sat down and saw the only people in Romford I'd noticed so far that day actually wearing suits. It was just a shame, I thought, that they had chosen trainers as their footwear. They were estate agents, Romford's white-collar community. Beside the door was a sign which read 'The management reserves the right to refuse entry or service to any customers'. If instead they'd stipulated 'anyone wearing trainers' they would be out of business.

Another thing that pissed me off about Romford was the way shops would shamelessly advertise deals in their window displays and then patently fail to live up to them. There were three music/video stores in the main street, all of which offered an exceptional deal on pre-recorded video cassettes. I was keen to acquire some new ones so was drawn in by the sign, which read 'Closing-down deal – everything must go – three videos for £10'. Can't say fairer than that, I thought. So I walked into the shop and discovered rows and rows of videos all priced at £9.99. I kept looking, and right at the back of the store was a shelf with videos at the advertised price, three for a tenner, including such hits as *German World War II Planes Revisited*. Cosmic.

As I waited for the train back to London later that day I saw a policeman, truncheon in hand, waiting on the platform opposite. It's a safe bet in Romford that any returning locals are thugs in need of being arrested.

As the train sped back to dear old London, I read in the *Essex Courier* of research by the Institute for Employment Services which claimed a trend towards people 'teleworking' – or working from home, as you and I would understand it – is putting 'a great deal of pressure on housing in the countryside'. This alarmed me: it smacks of a government looking for more reasons to justify rubber-stamping development programmes. I mean, if more people are working from home, why should there be a need for more housing in the countryside? Are so many people living in rotten urban housing that will not safely accommodate a laptop computer and a phone line?

Meanwhile I read a report in the sister paper, the *Romford Courier*, and the news became a little more credible. A Romford guy had had his ear severed after he was struck by a brick when he tried to pursue a group of youths who had just smashed one of his neighbours' windows. Discovering how rough the provinces all are had brought me to a desperately low point in my life. I thought I'd try somewhere else in the Home Counties which I hoped would be a bit tamer.

13. Watford

A frightened town

I was looking for a bit of light relief, and I was in for a disappointment. In 1838 a report from medical officers to the Union described Watford as being 'unhealthy', with 'three houses without a privy and an open dungheap and a slaughter house', according to *The Book of Watford*, published by Pageprint (Watford) Ltd. It continues, 'This was in 1838 . . . ten years elapsed [and] produced no improvement, nor is any likely to be produced.' Some things, as they say, never change.

I had never visited Watford before, nor had I had any plans to do so, not least because of its tiresome football club. But I went anyway, if for no other reason than I wanted to know what kind of place it was that made Nick Leeson so spectacularly arrogant. I was expecting to encounter a load of City traders, but this didn't happen.

It took over an hour to reach by the Underground, mostly overland. The journey reminded me of the days when I used to commute from the same end of the Metropolitan line in Northwood: tedious. At least I was travelling out of the rush hour and so could find a seat.

Watford Underground station itself is very conveniently located, provided you live in Cassiobury Park Avenue. Otherwise it's a good mile's walk from the centre, but an attractive one if you like looking at large Victorian houses with mock-Tudor beams, expensive thief-proof windows and burglar alarms. The avenue is a straight road about half a mile long with an abundance of trees and flowers. Off Rickmansworth Road is further evidence that Watford would be a rather better contender for Britain in Bloom than Southport, for there you find the well-tended and attractive Cassiobury Park itself.

But an avenue and a park don't really make a town. Bordering both of these is the Watford ring road, a dual carriageway which undulates beneath the ground and over subways. Step out of one such subway and you've suddenly reached the town centre. The first visible building is Yates' Wine Lodge.

Along the high street there are a couple of very smart looking restaurants. In all my travels through England's towns I had not seen even one restaurant that looked appealing. So was Watford going to turn out to be a bit of a waste of time; was there going to be nothing to suggest it had gone rotten? Quite the reverse – it stinks. Let me explain.

The tree-lined promenade in the centre of Watford looks incredibly smart, lined as it is with trees and expensive shops and lacking as it does litter. However, again – as I was later to witness in Cheltenham – one street does not make a town. Beyond the extremities of this one pedestrianised road, with its posh Oxfam and its stupidly named theme bars, Watford is no stranger to graffiti.

Pubs on the edge of the town centre are filled with impoverished locals all trying their best to talk proper. On the way to one such bar, after calling at a cashpoint machine, I was accosted by no fewer than three Irish women, all asking for 'money for the baby', all holding the same style of polystyrene fast-food begging trays, and only one accompanied by an infant, who looked about five. I refused politely, which is more than the cashpoint had done, telling me to get lost when all I'd wanted was a tenner. Still, I also paid in a cheque and when I mentioned that I had no pre-printed paying-in slips, the cashier automatically filled in all my details herself, which made a change from the instruction to go off and fill one out and join the back of the queue. Even Watford's *banks* tried to create an illusion of gentility.

The poorer citizens of Watford and its students support the town centre and its bars. The wealthy ones never drink in the town centre as they are too busy with work and a decent social life. But, ironically, both sides support the illusion of a wealthy town. The only appearance the wealthy seem to make in the town centre is when they pass through in four-wheel-drive cars.

The susceptibility of Watford to the same problems of violence and delinquent youth is in evidence everywhere, penetrating the disguise. The smashed-up sign of an insurance broker at the end of the high street was just one of many small but tell-tale signs that Watford is a frightened town.

It was time for a drink, but the characteristically slow bar service in Yates' led me to look instead for a drink in one of the town's stupidly named bars. As I left the immobile queue in Yates' I pondered its slogan. 'Often imitated', maybe. 'Never bettered' – I think not. I was to return for a second try later that day, when there was no queue but also no suggestion by any of the three chatting youths behind the bar that they had any intention of serving me.

I rejected the Ice Bar, which had the word 'Garage' in large letters in the window. I don't *have* a car. So instead I went to Artichokes, which I found was a good description of its customers. I found a seat, but it was directly beneath a loud-speaker blaring out a sports broadcast. I moved to the other side of the bar, but could not escape the annoying presenter who would periodically remind listeners of its quiz that day. 'Calls cost *just* 60p a minute,' he announced. Have they really found their audience, I wondered, leaving half my drink.

Outside, across the precinct, were two ten-year-old boys letting off crackers from two boxes of the things that I assumed they must have just shoplifted from Woolworths.

The front page of the *Watford Observer* warned its horrified readers that asylum seekers could be set to move in to Hertford-shire. Inside was evidence that the estates of north Watford cause the place as much trouble as those of Harrow. A report also illustrated the problem the town has of abandoned cars. A car seems to be a virtual necessity in Watford, unless you live in Cassiobury Park Avenue and can walk to the station. But even then it is half an hour's walk to the town centre. Another story reported that Watford had been knocked off the number-one spot of 'most expensive town to rent retail premises' by Cambridge.

So apart from a few streets with expensive houses, a ridiculous shopping centre and some rough estates, what did Watford have to offer? Rather sadly, it's a local obsession with its football club. Oh yes, even the local MP is reduced to persuading employers to allow their staff to turn up at work wearing the club's strip in aid of some charity or other. And it's customary for the letters pages to be riddled with stories relating to that bunch of sponsored Neanderthals who kick a ball around for the sake of a random score.

But what was on the lips of everyone there that day was the problem of travellers, or gypsies as they are known there. Just like in many other municipalities, there was a campaign in Watford against 'the gypsy epidemic'. Another report revealed how 'lightning action' by quick-thinking council members in nearby Abbots Langley had managed to get rid of 'a small band of gypsies' who had just been evicted along with their caravans from Watford's South Way playing field. A councillor congratulated his council's quick action, saying, 'It didn't give them time to create any rubbish. We're very pleased.' It's one kind of vermin against the other in Watford.

Apart from that, Watford's local press does not like to draw too much attention to the problems the town has of vandalism and itinerant youth, and instead leaves stories of this nature to the later pages, where one- or two-inch-long stories report on police appeals to witnesses of attacks on individuals by gangs armed with baseball bats. What is it with baseball bats? I didn't think the English *played* baseball.

Further on still was a report that the good old council was going to fell a cluster of ancient lime trees, as it deemed them to be a 'risk to the public'. A risk to building development, more like. At last I could see what it was that made convicted trader Nick Leeson so arrogant: it's a way of life in Watford.

Evidence of a prominent working class in the town was accidentally borne out in that day's *Watford Observer* by a report on the local fire brigade warning chip-pan users to exercise greater care, following a spate of related house fires.

Meanwhile, in the preface to the sequel to *The Book of*

Watford, cannily entitled *The Book of Watford II*, which covers the years 1960–96, A.G. Dillingham (b.1910) writes, 'Wherever I go nowadays, the prime topic of conversation among the older folk is their dislike of the present Watford.' Watford itself is a story of failed rebellion and planning, and the results are amazing. It's clearly a frustrating place to live, for whatever remains that is pleasant about the place is under constant threat of redevelopment. The green belt has all but disappeared, or is about to do so.

The 1950s onwards have seen the mass destruction of Tudor buildings in the area, as they stood in the way of the Disney planners. And with them went a load of amazing old pubs, which include:

The Dog (1720–1969) – demolished to make way for a student car park

White Hart (*c.*1600–1974) – demolished to make way for the hideous ring road

Eight Bells (1725–1954) – now a NatWest bank

Green Man (1730–1975) – demolished

Kings Head (1600–1961) – demolished

Leathersellers Arms (1680–1960) – demolished

Rose and Crown (*c.*1500–1968) – demolished

Spread Eagle (1750–1958) – demolished

Three Crowns (*c.*1600–1958) – demolished

I'd had enough. I gathered my souvenirs, hiked back to the station and boarded the first train back to London, passing through the slums of west London such as Harrow. Metropolitan line trains, while a lot cleaner than those of the mainline service, resemble fairground rides. I arrived home and threw up.

14. Stevenage

*A nice place if you like hideous architecture and
don't mind getting beaten up*

The idea for including Stevenage in the book came from a number of people who have or have had the misfortune to live there. They promised I would not be disappointed, and sure enough I was not. 'It's a nice place if you like hideous architecture and don't mind being beaten up,' a guy named Pete told me. This was enough for me – I was on the next King's Cross to Stevenage train.

Stevenage's train station is one of England's least attractive and leads at one end to a leisure centre and at the other to a car park lined with US-style eating houses.

For once I travelled with my wife, of whom I'd seen very little over the past few months. Well, I'd been off exploring places I'd never wish to see again, making friends with local councils and generally submerging myself in deep depression. My wife hadn't seemed to believe much of what I had said about England's provincial towns. By that stage she hadn't seen much of the country outside London. That day she was in for a shock.

She had looked so sweet, sitting forward on the train seat staring with childlike fascination at the passing view from the windows as we sped towards our destination. We arrived shortly before noon. By lunchtime her make-up was running.

A few miles short of Stevenage, the train had passed through Knebworth. My wife pointed to the mock-Tudor beams on the outside of a late-1990s building and, utterly perplexed, asked, '*Why?*' The last people able to mock the Tudors convincingly were the Victorians.

We wandered around for a while looking at the windswept car park which was almost empty. It was Saturday. Ahead we could see two tacky-looking nightclubs next door to each other, one called Vogue, the other one Pulse. Elsewhere was a cinema complex and a wide array of fast-food restaurants. And surrounding this complex were ICL, Magnet and other industrial warehouses.

This was the first clue we had to the fact that Stevenage is a place where a car is a necessity. The only entrance to this complex for pedestrians seemed to be the station. As we walked down the steps to the car park itself, we passed an undated weather-beaten sign which claimed that Boy George would be performing 'this Thursday'.

We'd skipped breakfast so, hungry, we ate in the 'Oriental Buffet'. Most tables were full but there still appeared to be more staff than diners. It made such a change encountering staff efficiency, and to top it all every one of them had a smile on his or her face, which helped to quell the disappointment I was to feel on finding that the food was all lukewarm.

My wife expressed her intrigue as she tucked into her chicken wings and chop suey. 'All the restaurants in the Midwest are like this, irrespective of the kind of food they serve,' she said as I stood up to refill my plate, obediently following the order of the restaurant and eating as much as I could. It had been a pleasure. Now we had to go and see Stevenage real.

We passed back through the station and on past the Corinthian Conference and Entertainment Suite, through the windows of which we could see an art gallery displaying pictures that looked as though they had been removed in the late 1980s as unsold stock from the shelves of a tacky department store, rejected by the new home-buying masses. 'Wizard in moonlight', 'Unicorn in moonlight' and 'Dragon in moonlight' seemed to be the main themes of the pictures on display. On the wall was a noticeboard with a newspaper cutting of a Labour candidate, described by my wife as 'wearing a dress I'd not even have worn in 1983'.

Ahead of us was the gateway to the town itself, and two signs. One warned of CCTV in operation, while the other pointed to the magistrate's court. To our left was the leisure centre, manned but empty.

But still we couldn't get into the town itself without passing through a busy marketplace. My wife, who had remarked on the lack of dress sense not just of the politicians but also of the locals themselves, sighed in understanding when she saw that all the clothes on sale were of the same appalling style (her words). What struck me, meanwhile, was that all the men, of whatever age, had tattoo-lined arms.

We found our way through to the town centre and gazed at the horror of it all: a sprawling concrete mass of 1950s idealism, with interconnecting subways. A kind of clock tower, whose purpose was to show the number of days remaining to the end of the year, had a plaque on one side which boasted of the achievements of Stevenage Development Corporation, 1946–1980. That's it, I thought – name and shame the buggers. Until 1946 the place had been a genteel and beautiful town. Now it is a run-down shopping centre which comes to an abrupt stop in every direction and which leaves stranded pedestrians with a choice between killing themselves on a major junction with dual carriageways which lead off to the miles and miles of north Herts new estates, or returning to the shops. We chose the latter.

The *Stevenage Mercury* ran a large story that week on how the local council planned a 'makeover' for what they called 'a tired-looking shopping centre'. One of the impetuses for the plans was that Stevenage apparently has 'fewer shoppers than any other town centre in Hertfordshire', is rated as low-quality by shoppers, and is in need of classy department stores. And – get this – the article cites a local councillor saying, 'It is easy to make a 300-year-old town look good, but more difficult when it is just 50.' What a load of *crap*, and an admission in itself.

There are plenty of job agencies in Stevenage town centre, and all the jobs appear to be for drivers, warehouse packagers or telesales assistants.

'These new towns are built so people can shop, creating a consumer society,' said my wife. 'Look – there's a wheelchair loan service.' I saw what she meant.

I took a look in the windows of a few estate agents. One displayed an abundance of three-bedroomed properties around the £70,000 mark, which suggested the only reason families lived here was because they could afford to. A listing of the local building firms showed no fewer than 30 companies in north Hertfordshire working hard at destroying what's left of the countryside by erecting identical houses for the masses. All but two of these had the word 'Homes' as the second half of their title, resulting in, for instance, the name Bogus Homes.

We were wandering round in circles. There was no way out for us apart from by bus or taxi, unless we followed one of the multitudinous cycle paths which led to the new estates. That day, as it happens, I didn't see a single bicycle.

It would have been nice to have found more than just the one pub, a dismal working men's pub overlooking the bus station which at 3 p.m. that day offered standing room only, its seats occupied by drunk old men and younger men in matching nylon shirts and trainers. The lack of shopping bags suggested this was the class of people who spent their money on drink rather than in the shops, which since the late 1940s has been all that's on offer. The leisure centre might have seemed a good idea at the time, but it costs money to join. The most noticeable group of people in Stevenage are those who aren't prepared to spend this cash on the kinds of leisure on offer.

We left our drinks and found an obliging taxi driver to take us on a tour of Stevenage. He drove us first to Stevenage Old Town. This was a stretch of road a quarter of a mile long which, he told us, was what the whole of the town had once been like: attractive old buildings interspersed with inviting old and unspoiled Tudor pubs. 'I wouldn't recommend walking round here after 9 p.m.,' he warned us, just as I was beginning to think there was a nice part to Stevenage. 'See those estates – the kids who can't afford the leisure centre come down here after dark to mug whoever they see.'

He had three children, he said, and his biggest nightmare was watching them grow up attending 'the most appalling schools'. 'Unless you're Catholic or can afford private schools, your kids don't stand a chance,' he said.

We left the Old Town and entered the first estate, passing by parking-free allotments and pebbledashed council houses before turning on to a road which seemed to go on for miles and which was lined with cheap 1960s and 1970s houses which made most council properties look attractive in comparison. 'About 90 per cent of Stevenage is like this,' the taxi driver said as we drove on and into a council estate called Bedwell. 'This is rough, but not the roughest estate. I'm not driving through there.' On our left was a grim-looking pub built at the same time as the surrounding council flats. I'll say one thing about Stevenage, though – there is an abundance of trees which disguise the rotten nature of the housing which goes on without relief for miles and miles and miles.

Then, as suddenly as Stevenage Sabotaged Town had ended, we were driving past bigger, detached houses. They were all identical and the typical dwelling among these was one whose 400-square-foot garden was overlooked by 40 windows. At the start of these was the obligatory new pub. 'Don't go there after 9 p.m. either,' the taxi driver warned us. We had no intention of doing so.

15. High Wycombe

Even the yobs are pretentious, using golf clubs rather than baseball bats as weapons

High Wycombe puts the dormant in dormitory town. It's Newestatesville with a virtually disused marketplace. A map of the town is a shapeless black-and-white line drawing of cul-de-sacs.

I travelled there from Marylebone station, to be greeted at High Wycombe station with news that I had travelled on the 8.07 from Marleybone. I stepped on to a platform of pushy, miserable commuters awaiting the next train to London. The only voices I heard were ones complaining about the parking, the trains or other factors which made their lives even more miserable – as if being themselves was not enough.

Across the road from the station is the Welsh-looking Flint Cottage pub, and it is clear where its imaginative name comes from (though I have no idea how or why an apparent majority of the other pubs in High Wycombe have managed to acquire the title The Falcon).

It was in the Flint Cottage that, ten years earlier, I had had my first High Wycombe experience. My flatmate from college days who played in a band was performing on the promise of £400, which would cover the cost of hiring a van and the necessary equipment for the evening. In the event, a trainload of his friends and acquaintances, myself included, turned up to support him, multiplying the number of people in the pub that night several times. When his drummer was off relieving himself after the first encore, Brendan ad libbed with a Derek and Clive song. A few minutes later, their gear back in the car, the band approached the landlord for their dues. I was then treated to the spectacle of a belligerent landlord making up off the cuff an excuse not to pay my friend for the business he had pulled in that night. Like everyone else, I was incensed. So I had every reason to want a fuller picture of what High Wycombe people are really like.

But first I wanted to get to see the town itself. For a place which I was to find had such a high crime rate, the streets of the town centre were very quiet. Half the population had commuted to work, and most of the other half must have been in bed or counting their loot. The town centre is pedestrianised and lined with shabby shops occupying the spaces between Dixons, Marks and Spencer and WHSmith.

I eventually found a newsagent's, located bang opposite WHSmith. The Asian woman who served me asked if I was a student. When she learnt I was writing a book, she asked me how she could get her cooking book published. I told her to cheat. 'Tell the press you've already got a publisher,' I suggested. 'The publicity will help.'

We got talking and, as is so often the case in places like High Wycombe, the only genuine people, the only ones not stuck up their own backsides, seemed to be the Asians. She was most courteous and the first and last person I was able to strike up a conversation with that day. The rest I tried but they were either too interested in their own lives or just incapable of the art of conversation. They talk to themselves, but look at unfamiliar people as though they are insane, and certainly as though they are unwanted.

I noticed what she meant about students. There were hundreds of them all over the place, skipping lectures, and they were all dressed weirdly. By weirdly I mean sadly, with hair dyed yellow or pink. According to the *Bucks Free Press*, it's the students who commit a fair proportion of the local crimes, or at least they make up a high proportion of the ones that get caught. Their defence is to argue that a custodial sentence would set them back at the beginning of their glittering careers. What about the people they set back in the process of their criminal activities?

The people who do not leave High Wycombe by day really

are a thick bunch. All who served me apart from the Asian woman looked at their tills as a one-year-old would study a toy designed for a six-year-old. In one bar a nose-studded girl typed seemingly random digits for ages before giving up, rather like those infuriating people you always get in front of you at cashpoints apparently typing in a 300-word essay.

An overwhelming proportion of the news in Buckinghamshire, and particularly around High Wycombe, is about village stores and pubs closing, with blame levelled at the 'trendy young people' who move there 'thinking it's posh'. They may be referred to by the epithet 'snobs', but 'posh' they ain't.

I was not altogether surprised when I read a big news story in the *Bucks Free Press* that day about the 'haemorrhaging' of manufacturing jobs in the High Wycombe area. Opposite was a fairytale headline: 'Smelly toilets put people off town.' Kind of summed up High Wycombe. Of course, there was the usual story crime-ridden provincial centres get in their weekly papers about an 'urgent need' for more CCTV cameras. So the criminals will relocate. Even the yobs in High Wycombe have pretensions to being a cut above their counterparts in other areas: they use golf clubs to beat people up, rather than baseball bats.

The local property guides reflect the standards of bullshit that prevail in that part of the country. You can pay £600,000-plus for an ugly new house. The Home Counties have become one mass of self-illusion and greed.

The tourist office was busy, but I felt sorry for those who'd hiked all the way to see a market square whose most notable feature was a plastic-clad ten-year-old reproduction of the Chepping Wycombe Improvement Act 1874 with a list of market tolls. The tourist office itself actually charged me 75 pence for the most undetailed restaurant list I'd ever seen. This one had the names of the eating places and their addresses, but no detail as to what sort of food they might sell.

High Wycombe has aspirations towards being a market town and wishes itself to be another Harrogate, but in fact it is just a dormitory town in the commuter belt. It has a history of

furniture-making, but that seems to be long gone. Apart from tourists and drunks, there's virtually no one else to see on the streets. The place really has nothing of which to be proud.

I took the first train I could back to London, which was a slow one and stopped at a dozen places along the way. Beyond the shrubs and weeds growing alongside the railway line, I could see housing estates which have sprouted since the 1950s spreading in all directions. Soon farming will go the same way as furniture manufacturing in High Wycombe and mining in t'north, because there will be nowhere left to farm.

The first few stations we passed through *en route* to London's Marleybone showed signs of the decay that has halted civilisation in this country. Gerrards Cross has statues on the platform, offset by rather more prominent advertising hoardings. In between stations were car parks packed with four-wheel-drive cars driven by precisely the kind of people who are accused of destroying village life. These people are slobs and a sad feature of the demise of the English class system. Whom do the working classes emulate now? It's only prats like these, as the old landed gentry has been forced into even greater obscurity.

Trains on this particular service displayed a warning of a kind I'd never seen before and it quite shocked me: 'Please keep all your personal belongings with you at all times.' What if you needed the loo? It had never crossed my mind that on going to the buffet car or taking a leak, I might be robbed on a train. Except in Spain, of course.

We passed on through a deserted Denham Golf Club, followed by Denham itself. The place looked like a builders' site, with a canal and a yacht club in the background. Here were more of those who destroy the countryside, not least by creating a demand for ugly rural housing.

16. Gravesend

*Like so many English 'seaside' towns, Gravesend is not
an obviously beautiful place*

The train was packed with passengers alighting at Charing
Cross, where I went to catch a post-morning-rush-hour train to
Gravesend. Many of the arrivals looked tired and were carrying
black bags as their luggage. These weren't Connex South-East
cleaners, either. By contrast, when I boarded this same train for
its return to Kent, the carriages were almost empty. I wondered
if those I'd seen disembarking were refugees fleeing Kent for the
last time.

Of the few who were on the train going back to Kent, most
were young people going home to their Dartford or Gravesend
homes. The children were a frightening breed, all of them
wearing wasp-like tracksuits, and most of the boys wore earrings
and had premature footballer fringes to disguise the onset five
years hence of a receding hairline.

The train trundled on through the atrocious mess of south-
east London, at one point the tracks actually passing through the
middle of a tower-block estate with burnt-out, smashed-up and
stolen cars decorating each building's surroundings. This view
dominates the entry to Kent and carries on well into the county
itself, uninterrupted by any sign of countryside or of architecture worth mentioning. Instead there are more smashed-up
cars and run-down council estates littering the view for miles
and miles, punctuated every now and then by gas cooling towers
and factory warehouses.

The train paused at a place named Belvedere. I glanced out
of the window and said a little prayer of thanks for not having
to disembark there, where the view was conspicuously not a fine
one.

Indeed, much of Kent itself is an eyesore. From Woolwich onwards there are hundreds of new estates built with a life expectancy of 20 years. Slade Green looked more like Slade Prison and I certainly couldn't see any green. A few hundred yards on and the railway embankment disappeared for a short way, opening up the view of a countryside littered with box houses built in the last 30 years. In the last ten years every remaining available space had been filled in with newer models.

It amounted to an hour of passing by nothing but ugly houses wherein must dwell a significant percentage of the UK's supposed 58 million or so residents. Dartford's view as far as the horizon was grey and industrial poison, and in the vicinity of the station itself by the trackside were old mattresses and furniture sticking out of the litter. It was difficult to spot where housing estates ended and car breakers' yards began.

Greenhithe for Bluewater station was a ridiculous name for a polluted dung heap, Swanscombe was a mass of industrial chimneys, warehouses and cranes, while in the surrounding countryside pylons outnumbered the trees.

Finally we reached Gravesend, which is actually an anagram of Arse-end, bar a couple of superfluous letters. The centre of the town looks like the roughest part of others I have seen which themselves have been no better than refuse dumps. It lies in the shadow of a looming grey civic centre. The Anglesea shopping centre, meanwhile, lies on the ground floor of the multi-storey car park and looks like a 1950s experiment gone badly wrong but which has been left because nobody could be bothered to get rid of it.

I was on a quest for a drink to damp down the local dust and dilute its unpleasant vapours, but after 20 minutes of unsuccess-fully searching for somewhere moderately salubrious to drink in, I thought 'Come back, theme bars' as I stuck my head around a series of lousy, unclean and noisy Gravesend pubs. Then at last I found one. It *was* a theme bar, but had been taken over by old gits – loud, smoky, seventy-something miserable buggers who come from a different age and whose life is dedicated to pissing everyone off. I managed to stay for a quarter of a pint before the shouting began to hurt my ears.

Further down the road was the Riverside bar and restaurant, which looked appealing, and where I thought I might be able to find a bit more from the locals about the history of the town. It was gone noon, but the whole place was closed down. Opposite was a bar called the Pier, labelled 'Irish House', which was also closed – although it did have a weathered old sign which read 'Irish bar opening soon'.

I returned to the town centre. It'll take a lot more than a few hanging baskets to make that place attractive. I bought a local newspaper, the *Gravesend Reporter*, whose front-page lead story was written in posthumous sympathy for a suicidal arsonist who had thrown himself off the multi-storey car park. *Sympathy*, for Christ's sake! What kind of a message is that sending out to other local suicidal arsonists?

Other pages recorded race attacks, gangs of elderly people's bag snatchers, depressed burglars and, of course, the usual Save our Hospital campaign. Don't these people realise that's how Blair's feel-good factor *works*? You *feel* good, so you don't *need* treatment. Honestly, some people are never satisfied.

I was peckish, so when for a change I went into McDonald's again for reason other than simply to use their loo, I spent half an hour queuing for a cheeseburger surrounded by screaming young people with no manners at all. They were all setting a particularly bad example to their offspring.

In the tourist office I was told that all the historical inform-ation as to where the town got its name would be in the free literature I could take away. Well, I read every word of the glossy pages I was given and was left none the wiser. But at least Gravesend *had* a tourist office; neighbouring Dartford's tourist office closed two years earlier.

Gravesend has a rich supply of single-lane and frantically busy one-way streets which can make crossing the road an extremely time-consuming process. I was later to miss my planned train back to London thanks to one such road opposite the station with no pedestrian crossing or junction in sight.

Around one in 20 vehicles in Gravesend that day seemed to be a truck towing a burnt-out vehicle. I couldn't remember having seen any such vehicle before, so to see so many in one day in one town suggested something was wrong with the place. Between these were ringed Ford Escorts with mismatched doors, nodding dogs, tattooed drivers and obese and ugly girl-friends.

I was approached for a light by an unwashed ten-year-old with a smaller friend. They were the spitting image of the children who killed young Jamie Bulger. They left after I'd obligingly produced a lighter, to retake their seat on the railway wall from which they had been throwing debris at passing trains. It interested me that for a town so filled with patrolling policemen and policewomen, as I had noticed in the shopping centre, there were no figures of authority prepared to put up any objection to what these budding young car thieves were doing.

From what I overheard in the Railway Tavern, most of Gravesend's youngsters have a criminal record by the time they reach their twenties, so of course the courts have to be lenient. Reports of court hearings that week suggested that if sent to prison, an overwhelming number of these criminals would be neglecting their elderly parents for whom they have to care. It seemed most unlikely, seeing them that day. Does nobody ever check defence allegations?

Of course even the name Gravesend has a funereal ring to it: a dead town, at the very end of the line. But if it is haunted, it also has features that are haunting and even unexpectedly exotic. It is the burial place of Pocahontas, for a start, as the Princess Pocahontas Gardens, the Pocahontas Coffee Shop and other eponymous attractions tirelessly remind you. In the recent Disney version she decided to stay in her native land to find herself and commune with the trees, but in reality she was buried somewhere in the chancel of St George's Church, Gravesend, under the prosaic name of Mrs Rebecca Rolfe.

If arriving by train, head north into the town centre and visit the Pocahontas Gardens and St George's Church just behind Princes Street. The church is a lovely cool, airy building completed in 1733, set in a quiet leafy square, and the Pocahontas connection is again vaunted: don't miss the two memorial windows in the south aisle to the tragic heroine, donated by the splendidly named Society of Colonial Dames of America in the State of Virginia. The gardens contain a rather touching statue of the girl, forever looking seaward, her back turned on the England that probably killed her with a little dose of the plague.

While the Pocahontas story is an obvious tourist attraction for some (if not, apparently, for most of the kids brought to admire her remains in St George's Church – they prefer McDonald's and the leisure centre), I was pleased to find some echoes of Gravesend's seagoing past still surviving. Like many English seaside towns it is not an obviously beautiful place – certainly not one for sailing types and G and Ts on pretty white yachts – and its atmosphere is that of a maritime museum rather than an active seaport. But it still has its old town pier, in a state of repair which may be politely described as picturesque, home to hundreds of birds and gently crumbling into the river Thames opposite the port of Tilbury.

The river's edge is a messy mudlarks' paradise, a strip of shingle and wide mudflats, the air humming with the throb of distant diesel engines, the ground littered with rusting iron and ropes and bottles of Brazilian pineapple juice and Dutch shampoo. Out on the river there are more little boats to look at and admire – *The Swiftsure*, *The Sussex* – while out in the middle channel a vast container ship is coming into Tilbury, labouring under the pretty name of *The Sapphire*, although someone has at least tried to paint it sky blue. Opposite, on the Essex side, the sky is spiky with vast steely container cranes like things out of *Terminator*.

One can only stand and stare and regret the death of such grimy, fascinating traffic on the London Thames. Continue past the Canal Tavern and you disappear down narrow lanes between wharves and welding workshops, populated by men Standing Around and Burning Things in Oildrums. You will probably feel in imminent danger of being press-ganged and decide you have gone far enough. But at least you may have seen enough to feel that Gravesend, unlike most of the other towns visited in this book, has not yet managed to bury all the evidence of its past.

If you remain to be convinced of Gravesend's strangely exotic atmosphere, try reading the first few pages of Conrad's *Heart of Darkness* before you go:

> The water shone pacifically; the sky was a benign immensity of unstained light; the very mist on the Essex marshes was like a gauzy and radiant fabric, hung from the wooded rises inland, and draping the low shores in diaphanous folds . . .

Now doesn't that sound exotic?

I had an extended wait for my train, thanks to Gravesend's pedestrian-unfriendly traffic, but finally made it out. Glancing out of the window as we passed through the disgusting debris of humanity that is Deptford, I thought that there were at least some saving graces to Gravesend. All the more so when, disembarking on platform six, I saw the little tinkers of that station playing their old game of closing the doors while 75 per cent of those wishing to travel were still trying to board the train. I suddenly felt *so* happy not to have to rely on overland trains for my journeys to work anymore.

17. Southampton

The city that is 'leading the south'.
Where – into the English Channel?

One way, I discovered, of reducing the levels of distress caused by passing on a train through the shambolic network of cul-de-sac housing that has become the southern English countryside is to take refuge in a South-West Trains smoking section. The company that runs these tardy vehicles has abandoned the provision of entire smoking carriages and instead allows passengers who wish to inhale to do so in the buffet bar. (They've also abandoned the buffet, providing instead an occasional trolley service.) Designed rather like the first-class bars that were upstairs on 1970s jumbo jets, the 12-seat bars on these trains have small, cabin-like windows whose borders effectively limit one's view of the continuous destruction.

On its way to Southampton the train stopped at Winchester, a station which bore a massive sign: WELCOME TO WINCHESTER, HOME OF HAMPSHIRE COUNTY COUNCIL. As if anyone cared. Said council has recently been busy approving planning permission, I noticed, for wherever there are no rambling and tasteless extensions of its towns, the entire county is riddled with 'villages' which lie within forests of more of these buildings. House building seems as rampant and destructive as the Black Death, the difference being that we were able to get rid of the latter.

Occasionally there would be a small village surrounded by grazing livestock. Their days are numbered, I thought – both the lifestyle of the villagers and the land on which the livestock grazed. There really does appear now to be an unbroken chain of housing all the way from London to the south coast of this country.

Then suddenly we were in Southampton, or the airport, anyway. That made a change, stopping at a regional airport-serving railway station and not seeing the word 'London' in its title. But all you see in Southampton is warehouses and leisure centres and shops and nothing else. From the train, anyway.

Walk a few yards out of the station and you are confronted with a road junction the size of an international rugby pitch. Such a road layout would not look out of place in the capital, but for a piddling series of shopping centres such as Southampton is these days, with a population of 200,000 rather than ten million, it seems a bit pathetic. Especially as the prototype computer-controlled traffic system installed to link all the junctions is so phenomenally bad. Consultancy firms could hardly have implemented anything less able to perform its promised function within the public sector. The amount of space wasted with this particular junction could house 40,000 people and have 100 interconnecting streets if it were to be put to use by any competent council (if such there be).

The traffic sits at each set of lights at the junction, revving to go, and you could play the best part of a game of rugby before any starts to move. Like nocturnal creatures on rural A-roads, cyclists have come to recognise the time when all the lights are red as being a safe time to go out and play on the junction with no fear of being hit by a moving vehicle.

I got talking to a cab driver, who said, 'The thing about Southampton is that the city is constructed around traffic lights and the place is midway through a computer-controlled traffic-controlling test. Look – there are these digits which supposedly tell you where you will find ample parking in the city. Trouble is, the system is so bad that by the time you reach the place where you had been told to expect 87 parking spaces, they've all been taken. They call it a 'virtual parking' system. I call it crap.' Maybe it's just short for 'virtually no parking'.

I reached the centre. Of course, the first pub I saw was Yates' Wine Lodge. Who's bribing whom, I wondered, to make this the place that exists in the centre of every bloody English town and city? But I went in. I bought a pint and was brought the wrong drink, and while the problem was being sorted out I got talking to a sympathetic middle-aged businessman who was used to the service. He was angry with Southampton himself because the day before he had booked a conference room in the local Trusthouse Forte hotel, for which he had paid £35 a head. He described the events that had put him off Southampton for life: 'We had our three-hour meeting and went to an adjoining room for lunch. I'd ordered sandwiches. A guy came in with a tray of sandwiches. He took off the cling film and turned to leave. I asked him what we were getting in the way of drink. He said nobody had ordered *drinks*. Exasperated, I pointed to everyone around me and asked if he thought they might like something to drink after their long meeting. He frowned and left. Fifteen minutes later he returned with a jug of diluted orange squash and a jug of water. "Glasses?" I asked. "Oh," he replied, and wandered off to return with 50 or so plastic beakers. You could have filled all of them, provided you'd only put a drop in each.'

I took his point, finished my pint and left.

Every now and then you see a message from Southampton's city council claiming that it is 'leading the south'. Where – into the English Channel? It really is a load of hogwash.

Talking of which, I ventured thirsty into the Hogshead, again a hardwood-based national chain of mock-tradition theme pubs. It beckoned me with an advert for Boddingtons at £1.45 a pint. Frugally, I ordered a half-pint, for which I was charged 85 pence. Do I get a maths A* for spotting the anomaly between advert and actual service?

Southampton is sadly completely overrun with shops. The centre of the city has a grid of small parks, but they are surrounded by shopping malls, shopping centres and single shops which are either open or in the process of 'relocating'. To where, they never say. It struck me that more than just a few couldn't bring themselves to admit they were bad businesses which had in fact folded. The West Quay Shopping Centre, adjacent to West Quay Park and Leisure World, was according to the tourist literature at that point England's 'largest in-town shopping centre under construction'.

It then hit me that here, at the very edge of England, the people of Southampton had lost any concern they might have had over the difference between fantasy and reality. A mediaeval *wool* warehouse houses the *maritime* museum, and the *aviation* museum is based at *Ocean* Village. Okay, so Spitfires might have sunk, but there is no ocean connected to mainland Britain.

I was denied the chance of looking through Southampton's council-sponsored restaurant guide because, I was told, a new one was in the process of being produced. 'The current one is at least two years old. Most of the places have closed down or moved. The new one will be out soon,' said the woman in the tourist office. *Two years?* I've been dining out in restaurants in London for ten years and apart from Le Tier Bouchon in Soho I cannot off the top of my head think of any that have closed, let alone moved. Still, her refusal to relinquish an out-of-date review to a journalist marked a regard for reality uncharacteristic of Southampton.

I went and bought a cup of coffee and sat to read the tourist literature. It painted a sad picture. 'Southampton is fast becoming recognised as one of the south's leading nightclub cities,' it claims. I can just see them all flocking from Kent and Cornwall to dance the night away in a tacky Southampton Marina nightclub.

Oh, for heaven's sake – in exaggerating the attraction of the 'eateries' of Southampton, the town guide reports, 'Subway is the latest sensation in sandwich bars, an idea brought over from the USA, where your sandwich is made to order from fresh ingredients.' It's *years* since I ate a stale sandwich. It was on British Rail in the 1970s. That's the tone of Southampton City Council, congratulating itself on the most trivial of achievements. 'Look – we've built some shops! And they *work*!'

I bought the local paper, the *Daily Echo*. John Humphrys would have had a field day. It was crammed with the most pathetic local news stories. The lead story was the dubious account of a teenage female karate student who, she *alleged*, fought off a nondescript middle-aged man when he moved to attack her. 'He fell over, then fled.' I *love* an unsubstantiated story on a quiet week in August. Of course, the picture was of her kicking out at the cameraman. That was about the only piece of 'news' in that day's edition, unless you count the award given to Southampton's railway station.

I'm attacking the citizens of Hampshire rather than criticising the local press. After all, they presumably know what it is their buyers want to read. Clearly none of it is to be about what a gruesome part of the world it is in which they all live. However, if you want national news, you'll find it printed at 90 degrees to the rest of the text in a 'Stop Press' column at the foot of the page.

I walked on down between shopping centres to find myself being deafened by the sound from the excessively powerful loudspeaker next to a small yellow stage erected and sponsored by some local car-polishing company. Aimed at 'kids', the stage had been erected to attract under-16s who could go up and compete in anything from spinning a hoop to general knowledge (resulting in total silence from the competitors to such show-stoppers as 'Who was the last British Prime Minister before Tony Blair?'). It was soul-destroying to witness the crowd that had gathered in front of it, listening intently to the mindless bloke running the event who, in the style of an annoying DJ at a wedding reception, would come out with staccato bursts of banal comment every few seconds above the din of a female pop combo. The only reason I would have ventured any closer than I was, a hundred yards away, would have been to unplug the little git's amplifier.

I took a side road and walked through to another shopping centre extravaganza. The landscape was the same, but there was a bit of local variety. A Securicor van had its engine running, and the deafening continuous repeat of the announcement that the vehicle was in reverse was even more annoying than the git with the microphone down the road. There was another guy walking up and down the precinct with a banner which advertised a 'professional body-piercing service'. It might just as well have read 'The end of the world is nigh'.

I sensed someone somewhere in Southampton had a cooker

and I was hungry so, ruling out Burger King, I went on a quest for some lunch. I tried a theme bar (and, believe me, they're *all* theme bars in Southampton) named something like the Fat Cat. I asked the gormless youth behind the bar if I could pay for food with a Visa card. He pondered for a moment before saying blankly, 'You can only use Visa if you're buying food.' Five minutes later, when he'd comprehended the gist of my question, he directed me to the other end of the bar where a waiter would take my order. I'd have to order my drink from the waiter, too. I put up no objection and walked, cigarette in hand, to the dining area. It was a dedicated non-smoking section, so I walked out. My parents may object to this remark, but it *did* happen.

I resumed my search for food, not suspecting just how long it would take. I wandered around the centre for over a mile, passing only closed-down restaurants and thinking what a light read the next edition of the Southampton restaurant guide would actually be, before I came to a remote district of the town centre which had once been named, and was still officially called, the High Street. There were no adjoining shopping centres, so it and its commercial premises had fallen victim to the merciless nature of local planning. There I found no fewer than two restaurants, and both were open. This was a turn-up for the books, I thought, as I opted for the Chinese, which advertised cheap lunch deals.

All was going well – the prawn crackers, for a start, were fresh, and there was a large table with Chinese people themselves indulging in a bit of nosh. But then the soup arrived. Lightly flavoured boiling water. And I don't know what animal the alleged beef came from but it was not one with whose taste I was familiar. New Forest pony, I expect. That thought put me off the remainder of my main dish, but I wasn't missing anything. I know that I was buying cheap, but it really was not an acceptable excuse for something which tried to pass itself off as lunch.

As I left I turned and saw that the Chinese family were in fact relatives of the restaurant owners just scrounging a free meal.

Their three young children were absorbed playing hand-held computer games.

Hardly stuffed with lunch, contrary to my mission, I headed off to see what Historic Southampton had to offer. That afternoon I found a remarkable blend of old buildings, all of which seemed to have received the Southampton treatment. There were twelfth-century pubs which had been rebuilt a hundred years ago; there was a Tudor house museum which boasted a Tudor garden, which on closer inspection dated back to 1979 and whose exterior wall at the back was grey pebble-dash; and the Duke of Wellington pub claimed to have first been opened in 1490 (I didn't know he was present at the battle of Bosworth Field). In the same quiet area of town was a bar called the Atlantic Queen, describing itself as 'the most friendly pub in town'. It had closed down, but I saw where it got its name when I noticed the piles of *The Pink Paper* that had been deposited on its doorstep.

As I headed to the station I saw a full National Express coach turn the corner ahead of me. Its destination was Portsmouth. In the front seat next to the driver was a uniformed National Disgrace employee with metal studs protruding from his shaven head, who had his feet up on the adjoining seat and seemed to be midway through telling the driver a joke.

'A great city' Southampton may once have been. I just wish the local council wouldn't insult visitors by trying to tell them it still is.

18. A Heart-of-England Rover Ticket

I must have been the first person to have bought a Rover ticket since the railways were privatised three years earlier if it's true what I was told by the guy at Paddington station's information desk. My next trip was to take me through the Midlands and on up to Yorkshire.

It seemed a bit of a long shot, but I was trying to save on the cost of my journey, hoping it'd be cheaper than buying a series of one-way tickets. I explained why I was taking such a complicated route – that I was travelling through the arse end of England to write a book about it. The Rover ticket which he told me I should buy said otherwise, claiming instead to cover me for off-peak travel through the 'Heart of England'. Notably Stoke-on-Trent, Derby and a variety of pretentious nonentities like Cheltenham and nightmares like Gloucester.

'You've done well to ask for this. Haven't sold any of these for years. Saved yourself a lot of money you have,' said the salesman at the ticket booth as he handed me the multi-journey train pass. He had at first claimed the journey couldn't encompass Stoke, but he persisted in his quest, to discover with jubilation that the information desk had more up-to-date records and better software, and that I could indeed include Stoke. He turned out to be the first and last helpful Railtrack employee I would encounter that week.

Travel writing might sound like nice work if you can get it. That's all very well, but as I had pointed out to the cab driver who took me from home in Bethnal Green to Paddington, his envy was misplaced: this was not going to be a trip I would enjoy. I was going to venture once more into the wilds of England, far from the comforts and familiarity of the capital. Deliberately setting out to experience the horror of modern England, I would be stepping into a land where pubs still close at 2.30 p.m., where population centres are so small that anyone wanting to stand out will do so without much effort and with an incredible degree of misplaced self-importance, and where, by *law*, you cannot hail a passing taxi. I was to see more of a land where ancient buildings in town centres are judged by county councils to be nothing more than a hindrance to the development of yet more shopping centres.

Understanding the purpose of my journey, as the cab driver dropped me off he wished me bad weather, and I appreciated the gesture. Clear blue skies and sunshine would absorb much of the impact of what I was expecting to describe.

Most English citizens recognise that the country is decaying, but this is seldom documented other than occasional and ineffectual whimpering about the criminal destruction of hedgerows or the growth in youth crime. My plan was to point out a few more home truths about the fragmentation of England's towns and lifestyles. There doesn't seem to be much official objection to the hundreds of massive building firms storming through what remains of the English countryside erecting countless thousands of identical-looking houses.

Anyway, despite the success with the cheap ticket, my experience that first day wasn't altogether painless even before I had made it out of London. Before being served at the advance-travel counter at Paddington, I had to endure the time-consuming and vowel-less whingeing of a New Zealander demanding a ticket to 'The Cotswolds'. The ticket assistant explained he would need to know what destination he required. 'Just a t'cket to the Cotswolds,' the Kiwi 'ns'st'd. He was finally offered a 30-day Cotswolds train pass, but th's was not what he want'd, he said, as he was only going for three weeks. I wept.

The very first train I caught was packed and there were only vacant seats left in Coach B, the smoking carriage near the front. As the train pulled out of Paddington, like the first cuckoo came a familiar feeble voice: 'Oh, God, this is smoking . . . this is the smoking carriage . . . the rest of the train's full . . . Oh, God . . . Oh, GOD! It's disgusting . . .' syncopated with the sound of the train's undercarriage.

A twenty-something woman led her unfortunate and presumably long-suffering boyfriend back through to the next carriage to stand. I hoped their journey was going to take them all the way to Cardiff.

Half a mile further on came the second guaranteed feature of intercity travel: the non-smoking stragglers who finally find vacant seats. A youth of about 13 called back to his family, 'Dad! There's plenty of seats in here.' As the rest joined him, I looked at my watch. It took eight seconds for the musty scent to provoke expressions of disgust. So the buggers would have to stand at least until Swindon. I chuckled.

I accepted a Benson and Hedges offered me by a fellow passenger. Two non-smokers had occupied the seat behind me. Non-smokers are such windbags. So I carefully directed long plumes of smoke through the side of my mouth which would drift successfully through the gap in the seats to Mr and Mrs Fucking-Miserable. (They would presumably have adopted a double-barrelled surname to convince everyone that their ancestors were bastards too.)

Swindon had originally been the first stop on my itinerary. I changed my mind after thinking I couldn't include quite such an easy and obvious target to write about in the context of a decaying civilisation.

But then I reached Gloucester.

19. Gloucester

*If there was ever anything good to say about Gloucester,
it's dead and buried now*

It was a Saturday, so the Severn Bridge was closed for repairs.
This affected trains using the Severn Tunnel, which worked to
my advantage as it meant I could catch a Wales-bound train
which had been rerouted via Swindon and Gloucester. Otherwise I would have had to change at Swindon and the journey
would have taken longer. However, it did not seem to help
anyone else on the train that day. They all wanted to disembark
in places like Newport, Gwent (and Cardiff, Wales, as my
American wife would say) and most seemed concerned at the
route the train was taking. They certainly hadn't been told.
What once was British Rail seems to assume a lot of its passengers. Tolerance, mainly.

Gloucester's railway station is a three-minute walk from the
city centre – or no less than five quid in a cab, as the ring-road
system is so much more complicated than it really should be. It's
like modern Surrey, a tarmac vendor's idea of heaven, imprison-
ing pedestrians within the shopping district. How such a dreadful layout has come about is beyond me, and in such a small
place too. One forgets about these provincial idiosyncrasies
when one lives in the capital. County councils all appear to have
a passionate desire to establish ring roads interwoven with one-
way streets around their shopping districts. And shop is all
provincial Englanders seem to *do* these days.

Immediately outside Gloucester station, overlooking the car
park, is an inn displaying an unfeasibly large red banner which
advertises accommodation from £15 per night. This has been
hanging outside the front of the building, dominating most
people's first impression of the place, ever since the early 1990s

when the city was profiting from its only modern tourist attraction, the sensational and depraved Fred and Rose West multiple murder case.

Straight off the train, I walked to the bar of that inn and asked the woman if there were any spare single rooms for the night. She said something unintelligible but which sounded vaguely like she would find out for me. Yet she continued to serve, moving further along the bar and displaying no intention of pursuing my request. I saw her whispering something to a colleague, and the colleague looking doubtful. Without gesturing or even turning her head towards me, she began to serve another customer at the other end of the bar. I picked up my suitcase, walked to where she was pulling a pint and asked the question again.

'No, I haven't got any rooms spare tonight,' she said, without looking up. This was my welcome to Gloucester, where I would spend the following 24 hours being treated with contempt. I felt like an extra in a Mike Leigh film.

So instead I went to the cab rank and asked to be taken to a hotel in the city's centre. Five minutes into the journey and all of 50 yards closer to my destination, the driver had established the purpose of my visit. 'Well, you've come on the right day,' he said enthusiastically. Why could that be – was there some festival or other? Ur, no. Or *urr*, no, as they say in that part of the world. 'All day sport and drinking. Then the nightclubs,' he said by way of explanation. He then painted a picture of Saturday nights in the area I was set to spend a night in that made me wish I'd taken up the offer of a trip to Kosovo instead. I hadn't fancied ending my days making sharp contact with military hardware delivered by one of those bright American pilots, but now . . .

Gloucester, I was to find, certainly has a history, but it's *all* history, and that's not the function of this book. I'm studying the present, the arse end of our civilisation. Gloucester calling itself a 'beautiful historic city' is like Weston-super-Mare describing its beaches as 'sandy'.

Every couple in Gloucester's city centre on a Saturday seems to be aged twenty-something, many passing the day in bars with their junior offspring, most of them fighting – the parents, that is. The behaviour I witnessed in a pub named the Tailor's House reminded me of Spain, where an abundance of redundant machismo is permanently on display among the young adult males. The pub was named after the Tailor of Gloucester. The guy never seemed to have had much time for Gloucester, though – he was actually born in Gwent in 1877, moved to Gloucestershire in his teens and is buried east of Cheltenham in Charlton Kings. On the street outside the pub was a blackboard advertising its bar meals as 'Tailor-made for your appetite'. Oh dear.

As with the rest of the bars in Gloucester, the beer was undisguisably watered down. And in that bar I saw my first fly of the year. This was early April. Eight weeks were to pass before I was to see another.

Gloucester is a town where I expected to find a Woolworths and a Halfords, icons of the Cortina-with-spoilers-driving small-town dweller in the last fifth of the twentieth century. As it turned out, the two shops were next door to each other.

It's fitting that the only person I could find able to express a genuine interest in the place was the author of *Historic Gloucester: An Illustrated Guide to the City, Its Buildings, the Cathedral and the Docks*. Philip Moss was born there and is an archaeologist by trade. Don't get me wrong, I have nothing against archaeologists and I even once worked in an archaeological laboratory, sieving Neolithic snails from soil samples. But it's fitting that his interest in his native city is all subterranean, for if there was ever anything good to say about Gloucester apart from the cathedral, it's dead and buried now.

The tone of his book is typical of all west of England provincial centres: 'Gloucester has been variously described as "The gateway to the west" and "The crossroads of England".' Or to reluctant visitors these days as 'a waste of space'. The landlord of the Black Swan, the inn where I was staying that night, referred me to a recent story in a national newspaper which condemned Gloucester as the most bleak population centre in England. But other such treats were yet to come.

I was peckish. So I went into a Tudor pub in the centre of town which was displaying a large menu outside. The jukebox was playing Sting – or, to be more precise, variations on a theme by Prokofiev. The girl at the bar told me that despite the blackboards displayed on the street, which had enticed me inside in the first place, food was not being served until six. It was 5.10 p.m. 'Try Café René across the road,' she said. 'They'll be serving food.'

I stepped outside and looked back at the pub. Above the entrance was a historical plaque. Gloucester's fond of plaques. This one denoted that the place had been built in the early sixteenth century and had been the home of someone inconsequential in 1718. So Gloucester has always been thus. At that point I suddenly felt sorry for Lucy Partington, murdered by the Wests, who had lured her to Gloucester in the '70s.

Café René had everything going for it: its proprietor wasn't in fact French, it was bang in the centre of Gloucester and it was situated down a quiet Tudor alleyway which had once housed the original Crypt Grammar School, in 1512. (Grammar was once spelt 'grammer', if the plaque bearing this historical allegation is anything to go by.) It was stylishly furnished – even if the style bore no connection to Gloucester, with upturned wine kegs and wall-sized wine racks. And it was almost empty.

I approached the barman, hoping he would confirm that I could be served some food. My question was greeted with an abrupt and officious, 'No, sir. Not till six.'

I was starving, though. 'Peanuts?'

'No crisps or peanuts, sir,' he said gleefully. His attitude alone could have explained the complete lack of patrons in the bar, and I muttered this as I left. Unreasonable of me, you might say, but you didn't see the look of pleasure on his face as he denied me any sustenance. This was a bitter man, though he probably didn't serve bitter either.

I later learnt that Café René had been a bikers' pub until a couple of years before, when it had been bought out and stylised the way it was when I arrived. It had become an immediate success. However, within a matter of weeks, as is so often the case in the English provinces, it had been bought out again, this time by a large regional brewer. A further three weeks later it had lost all its individuality in everything but appearance.

I was told all this by the barman in the inn where I was by now staying, who had worked there prior to the second of the transitions mentioned above. Representative of his claims of deterioration was the fact that the bar staff there were more interested in procedure than service. Among its new rules was the fact that it was closed for food till 6 p.m. – in something that called itself a *café*. So it could be French after all. But no, its original owner was an Irishman who just happened to like *'Allo 'Allo*.

So, reluctantly, I went back to the other pub to stuff myself with peanuts and keep myself alive till the kitchens opened. The girl who had suggested the foodless café served me. She had obviously only done so in the hope of getting rid of one more customer. On encountering her for the second time, I asked for two bags of peanuts with a pint of bitter. She handed me a pint of watered-down ale and just one bag of peanuts, which she had by this time rung up on the till. 'No, *two* please,' I said politely, indicating the nuts. At that point her flimsy humane demeanour dropped and she cursed as she swung back round and stubbornly re-entered the order on the cash register. Traces of the genetic English reluctance were still there, I thought, buried under the other modern feature of blinkered arrogance that has replaced grace and humility, a feature inelegantly displayed by most English children born during or since the 1970s.

One weedy, spotty 18-year-old was so inconsequential that his feeble Gloucester lilt, ill-fitting white shirt and black trousers delayed my observation of the bunch of keys that hung from his belt – the bunch of keys proudly displayed by many of life's non-achievers. For him, life had peaked. He was posturing before a collection of what I assume were his friends, out from a hard day's graft at Halfords and Woolworths.

The gait of these Gloucester boys resembled that of a guy I

had met in a Hackney pub shortly before the trip. He had approached me and a friend of mine from college – sorry, *university* – and introduced himself by declaring he was out on the town by himself. He had cropped hair and an accent that sounded frighteningly as if it came from Essex. The Essex boy had bought himself a drink and returned to join us. Quite why, we weren't sure. I enquired about where he lived, and he told me he was from Romford. 'That's interesting,' I lied. 'I'm writing a book which depicts interesting places and the lifestyle of those who live there. If I were to buy you a drink, perhaps you could spare a couple of minutes to tell me a bit more about Romford?'

His face glazed as it strained to comprehend, then relaxed as he said in a broad Romford accent, 'It's Romford,' saliva jetting out of the corner of his mouth as it struggled to engineer the 'mf' in the middle of the word. There was a pause. '*Rom*ford.' The more he repeated it, the more his head bobbed up and down in conjunction with his protruding chin and the more he began to dribble. Fortunately, after such a strenuous, intellectually searching exercise, he had forgotten about the offer of a free drink. We finished ours and left.

And here in Gloucester were his provincial counterparts. Every bit as articulate but with even less imagination when it came to dress sense. All this in a Tudor pub in the heart of a city proudly described by the guy in the tourist-free tourist office as 'neatly sandwiched between the ancient Forest of Dean and the incomparable charm of the Cotswold hills'. Nice sandwich; shame about the filling. The local tourist-office manager had looked stunned when I'd said I was writing a travel book, and had then looked even more alarmed when I'd told him that I was including Gloucester, where I wanted a taste of the night life, the people and the town centre.

Anyway, I prepared myself to forgive Café René and returned out of hunger at 6 p.m. There were four bar staff on duty as I stood at the bar, again the only customer, awaiting service. The staff were discussing the evening's procedure. After at least a full minute's wait, during which I had received nothing more than a couple of impatient glances from the staff and certainly no indication that they were going to serve me, I turned and left, this time cursing them a little louder.

This left me with a dilemma. According to a restaurant guide I had picked up at the queueless Gloucester tourist office of 24 listed 'places to eat', there were only six actual restaurants in the entire city, and half of these were either Indian or Chinese. Under the heading 'Fast Food', the guide included Pizza Hut and KFC but left out McDonald's. This must have been one of the most thankless publications to have had to produce. In addition to the restaurants, most of which seemed to close at 7 p.m., in order for it to be padded out to more than a page the alleged guide had to include far more cafés, which included those at BHS, Woolworths and Boots.

Even so, it spoke volumes* about the city: unless you wanted a curry or a pub meal, you'd have to drive miles out into the surrounding countryside, and even then the mediocrity of the service and food to be found throughout Gloucestershire would more than likely make you regret bothering to get there in the first place.

But the guide to eating out in the city of Gloucester was either incomplete or simply out of date, I was to discover, as it had missed out an Italian restaurant where, in desperation, I ended up eating and where, bewilderingly, nothing but Spanish singers with guitar accompaniment played through the speakers.

There I was given a Gloucester welcome. It was just past 7 p.m. – I'd spent the last hour unsuccessfully scouring the streets for food – and I was the first to arrive for a meal that evening. By this time I had wandered the entire length of a main street running through the city to find just one open restaurant, the Golden Dragon Chinese restaurant. It displayed in its window a blown-up copy of a Cotswold newspaper with a restaurant review written in clumsy provincial English. The paper was wrinkled and faded, and I noticed it was dated May 1989, so it

---

* or at least a sentence

had already celebrated its tenth birthday. It made me wonder about the kitchen, as I resumed my quest for sustenance.

In the Italian restaurant I asked if there were any spare tables and was told I'd have to be finished by 9.30 p.m. I began to say I had every intention of doing so, when another waitress butted in with, 'No, 9 p.m.!' But I was starving and principles fade when survival is at stake. So I didn't walk out.

In keeping with its location, the restaurant did not serve dry white wine. On asking for it, I was treated like Gloucester low life, by Gloucester low life – as though I had asked if the chef's hands were unwashed when he cooked.

When the waitress collected my menu after I'd placed my order, she'd cheered up a bit. 'Thanks, mate,' she said, which might sound vulgar but, believe me, isn't by the standards in that part of the world. At that moment the guitar tune changed to a tortuous Spanish rendition of 'My Way'. Personally I would rather they had played The Sex Pistols' version, which at least incorporates some elements of rhythm, harmony, melody and music.

I gave a small tip – sadly not one that involved telling them to choose another vocation – and left. Standing outside in the rain-soaked street, I checked my bearings and was promptly shat on by a seagull.

I returned to the Black Swan, washed seagull shit out of my hair and walked back downstairs to the main bar, where the proprietor immediately called out, 'You see, Mr Murphy!' I looked up, startled. 'You could have had a good meal here. I saw you coming out of that Italian place across the road. Or you could have eaten in a marvellous French restaurant down the road.'

I was taken aback. I hadn't noticed, but what had prompted this afterthought was the proprietor of Café René leaving the Swan. I embarked on my tirade about the place to the inn-keeper. As I did so, the guy who ran Café René stood before me, intervened defensively, 'We're fully booked tonight,' and Swanned out again. Is he French, I asked. 'No, Welsh,' said the landlord. Well, he *acts* French. I'm sorry, but bars bought up by large breweries do not usually stand a chance. Genuine service is anathema to those who run them and is replaced by a management style of mandatory clinical ignorance deprived of courtesy. In this instance, if they were fully booked, firstly why had I been told food would be served at six, and secondly, when I had returned *at* six, why had all the staff ignored me instead of explaining to me that I would not get served that night? Christ, I sound like my parents.

After 8 p.m. on a Saturday the bars in the city of Gloucester start to fill up with young men in ironed shirts and fawn trousers with gelled-back hair. This seems to be the dress code of Gloucester's three or so nightclubs, and one I was to discover to be common just about everywhere outside London. This fashion has led to untold wealth among shareholders in such stores as Buy Rite and Burton's. Judging by the increasingly tough job with which Her Majesty's constabulary has to contend each week in the early hours of Sunday morning, the success of the 'smart' dress policy imposed by these nightclubs has been marginal.

Don't mistake that for an endorsement of the Gloucester police, though. They can never be forgiven for operating in such a way as to have been responsible – yes, *responsible* – for the death of the great Austrian philosopher Leopold Kohr. After one of many thefts of his work by youths from a nearby council estate which would dwarf some of the largest and most violent Liverpool housing estates, and coming as he did from Salzburg in Austria where 'Silent Night' originated, Kohr penned the ditty:

> The only one sleeping in heavenly peace
> Is the superintendent of Gloucester police.

The landlord of the Black Swan was in his mid-fifties and had been brought out of retirement by a lifelong friend who had persuaded him to move out of London and come and run that establishment which he had just acquired and whose decay he was planning to reverse.

His opinion of Gloucester? 'Strangest place I've ever worked. Few nice people, but lots of nasty ones . . . Been nowhere, done nothing, going nowhere,' he said, indicating the three ironed-shirt-clad loud-mouthed reprobates he'd just expelled, to threats of armed retaliation.

All the conversation of the patrons of Gloucester's public houses, I noticed, surrounds the planning of their weekends, which are simply passages of drinking punctuated by going home to change into shirt and trousers before proceeding to the nightclubs.

At around 8.30 p.m. a party of women claiming to be dressed as Mrs Mopp entered 'to get tanked up' prior to attending a fancy dress party. When I went to the gents' loo the noise coming from the next room along sounded like a girls' school playground, with shrieks penetrating the tiled walls.

As the demented young women stood lapping up attention from other locals at the bar, a chorus of high-spirited Gloucester farmers slurred the words to the Worzels' 1975 hit 'I've Got a Brand New Combine Harvester', oblivious to the fact that it was the likes of them the song was mocking.

Half an hour later the women left, blowing party whistles and laughing hysterically. I assumed they do this every week. It's their release from a drab world for a few hours. No doubt a significant proportion of them would end up in police cells the following morning, attempting to bail out their boy of the moment.

At closing time, as I sat in the bar discreetly typing up on my notebook computer my impressions of Gloucester, I looked over my shoulder on hearing a loud 'Goodnight, sir!' in a German accent. A Nazi war criminal living untraceably in Gloucester was leaving the bar, looking at me and drunkenly waving. 'You come to pubs to talk to people, not to play with a machine!' he shouted in command mode. I shrugged and continued. First good thing I've had to say about native locals all day: at least they're not German. A *Blackadder* quote has made its way into the *Oxford Book of Humorous Quotations*: 'Germans are a cruel race. Their operas last six hours and they have no word for "fluffy".' Just as the French appear to have no use for the word 'principle'.

The council in Gloucester is still trying, and not just by nature. In the tourist office I was stung for £2.50 to acquire a 66-page publication put out by a division of the local city council itself, entitled *The City of Gloucester*. One third of those pages were taken up with advertisements for accountants, banks, electrical supplies, sign manufacturers, transport and warehousing, vehicle parking, property development and water supplies, to list but a few. Just the sort of facilities a tourist might need if he planned a tour of the scenic delights of the West Country. The tourist office gave the book priority position among all the publications it had for sale. Advertising revenue alone will have more than paid for the cost of production of the self-flattering rag.

The brochure contained a list of 'companies which are now well established in Gloucester', which included Cheltenham and Gloucester Building Society, South West Joinery, West Midland Farmers and West Country brewer Whitbread Flowers (formerly Flowers). Oh yes, and the Bank of England. Forgive me once again, but is the Bank of England a company?

The rest of that particular page is given to describing the towns with which Gloucester is twinned: Gouda in the Netherlands, Metz in France ('the French city of art and culture' – just the one, then), St Ann's in the Caribbean, and Trier in Germany. 'The twinning of our city with such a rare and important community is greatly appreciated by the people of Gloucester,' rants the brochure. I'm no mathematician but surely the list makes them quintuplets. Also I hardly need ask your view on whether there is likely even to be a blip of appreciation among the city's residents that it should have such a German 'twin' – apart, perhaps, from those local schoolchildren who get to experience an exchange visit which takes them briefly away from the grim and perpetual helplessness of their home city while they are at an age too young to form any opinion on the Nazi attitudes displayed in Trier. Most of them probably couldn't even *spell* 'world domination'.

The text of the Gloucester 'tourist' brochure is entirely plagiarised third-form school-project material: 'Gloucester is an ancient city, rooted in history – but with all the elements needed to maintain a thriving buoyant business community . . . It is doubtful if any comparable English city has such beautiful, varied and interesting surroundings.' This claim is not only doubtful, It Is pure fantasy. Whatever was meant by it, the brochure was clearly missold to me. The reference to its surroundings serves to heighten the sense of alarm on setting foot in the rotten city itself. 'Henry II granted us our first Royal Charter in 1155, raising the city to equal status with London and Winchester.' Neither it nor its citizens seem to have lost such illusions.

Gloucester City Council may well take offence at my comments. Let them. They should have thought twice before making me stump up £2.50 for this disgraceful publication. Consider this a book review.

A few years earlier I had been to a press conference in the City of London held by the West of England Development Agency. Its purpose, it said, was to break to the world the news that the West of England was going for the dubious title of something like 'Britain's Biggest Business Base Outside London'.

The statistics they came out with at that conference were bizarre and very urban Gloucestershire, and they were announced as though they were being read from a first-former's school project which had scored D minus. 'Bristol and its immediately surrounding business districts make up an area of 12 million people,' it boasted. So one in four people in England live in and around Bristol, do they? I suspect they even believed it themselves. There's no end to the entertainment to be found in the West Country.

Back in London after the jaunt round the 'Heart of England', I rang the agency for the purpose of this book to see what the organisation had been up to and to establish whether they had amended their stated goals. Or at least I thought I had rung them. Directory enquiries automatically gave me a number, which turned out to be that of the Western Development

Agency. I was driven to describing in words of one syllable what I meant when I had asked to speak to the press office. 'Oh, you want to speak to Gary. He's not in,' said the girl on the switchboard. The organisation set up to promote industry in the West Country does not appear to have a publicity office. Why am I not surprised?

But then I discovered a plethora of other aspiring business sponsorship groups, most of them set up in the last ten years, some of which had since merged. These included the Western England Development Agency, which had merged with some similar-sounding body and had indeed been launched in London in 1995 and was therefore probably the one I was after. So I rang them. Did they have anyone who dealt with press or marketing enquiries, I asked slowly. There was a long silence. 'The lady who deals with our press releases is on another number,' I was told. I rang that and got through to an answerphone on which I left a message. I never heard back from her, either.

Perhaps they've woken up to the fact that nobody apart from them actually cares, that their inflated titles encourage the responsible press* simply to ridicule their methods and achievements, and that the only publicity they want now is the type that appears in £2.50 brochures available at any West of England tourist office. Or they know that any journalist is going to take the piss out of them.

Anyway, the Western Development Partnership is based mainly in Bristol, while the West of England Development Agency is based in five West of England counties including Gloucestershire and Somerset. I think.

---

* I know – there's no such thing

20. Cheltenham

Where?

I had been there before, some 15 years earlier. One thing in Gloucester's favour is that it is not Cheltenham, a disappointing by-product of The Creation around eight miles from the city of Gloucester and as much use to the country as homosexuality is to evolution.

Cheltenham supposedly used to be a pleasurable, genteel town dominated by the upper-middle classes, but this is certainly no longer the case – if indeed it ever was. It made it on to the tourist map only a couple of centuries ago when a natural spring was discovered, but only 600 visitors turned up each year at its peak and so it never really established itself as a tourist centre.

Mention Cheltenham to anyone who's not been there and you will usually hear a comment along the lines of 'Oh, *very* posh'. In fact the town is no more posh than a northern seaside resort. There are one or two expensive schools there, but otherwise life in the town nowadays is just as helpless as it is in Gloucester. It comes out ten times worse, though, through its constant efforts to pretend to be otherwise. One or two* of the streets in the town centre may be less unattractive, but it hangs on to this deep-seated pretence that it has something going for it. It has not.

For instance, during my visit I was to learn that it has so obviously harboured such a blinkered self-infatuation over the past 20 years that, by the time I arrived there on this trip, it had over-ridden all common sense and described itself on the signposts at the entrance to the town as 'Centre for the

---

* Just the one, the Promenade

Cotswolds'. It's not strictly speaking even *in* the Cotswolds. The Cotswolds are notable for their colourful native limestone buildings. To see any of these apart from the town hall and a few streets of so-called Regency buildings, whose stone was imported from the Cotswold hills, you have to drive several miles north or east of the town. Admittedly, some of these locations come under the wider 'Borough of Cheltenham' definition, but the town itself is an arse. It was almost as though a competition has been launched quietly by the local council to see how far it can go with the most outrageously misleading claims about what is essentially now no more than a satellite town for the industrial Midlands.

I could sense that in Cheltenham I was going to have a field day, albeit one bearing GM crops, so I decided to stay for a whole week. I wanted to get to the bottom of why its citizens could be so misguidedly proud.

The curious thing about the way Cheltenham gives itself airs is that visitors seem to be taken in by it and leave with a sense of having learned something. It doesn't enter their heads to question why, if this town really is in the Cotswolds, it has a distinct lack of the distinctive Cotswold stone characteristic of buildings in places like Chipping Campden and the rather more substantial, if still badly decaying, Oxford. It's true that the Cotswolds are shared between Gloucestershire and Oxfordshire, but apart from being located in Gloucestershire, Cheltenham is no more in the Cotswolds than Swindon or Bristol.

I discovered that pointing this out to those who live there is another matter, though. It invariably seemed to upset them, and understandably so: it would give them an identity crisis when they've become used to being told by their local council that they have something of which to be proud.

Even my wife, who took a shine to Cheltenham's rather large Boots and who had read the misleading literature, later argued forcefully with me, siding with Cheltenham. It was only after some serious research on the Internet, avoiding tourist literature, that she realised that Cheltenham can at best be described as 'close to the edge of the Cotswolds'.

'Bloody man doesn't know what he's talking about,' I hear Cheltonians complain. Well, that's Cheltenham for you. It's characteristic of their stupidity. They are the kind of inverted and ignorant people who, if you were to try telling them to continue using the word 'me' rather than 'I' when adding to the sentence 'give it to me' – such that it becomes, for instance, 'give it to *Kevin and* me' – they'll fold their arms and sulk and refuse to listen to reason, for that's not what their illiterate English teachers told them. Meanwhile they pay more attention to tourist information than to geography. Essentially the vast majority of the population of that town are such ignorant bumpkins that they don't generally *have* what can be termed an attention span.

Oh yeah – and on the subject of geography, why is the train station so far from the town centre? To spare visitors the ordeal of having actually to see the place? Or maybe it is just the fault of Dr Beeching. The town itself has GCHQ, which is hardly a tourist attraction, and it has pump rooms dating from the town's days as a spa centre a couple of hundred years ago. There are also some quite nice houses on Queens Road, where the station's main entrance and car park are situated. But the rest of the town mostly is a dump.

Do you recall a phrase from the dim and distant past to the effect that 'The customer is always right'? Whatever happened to it? I'll tell you: it has been replaced with 'customers are a nuisance' – and who can blame shop assistants for adopting such an attitude when such a high proportion of their customers display a hideous and embarrassing blend of arrogance and ignorance that is just pleading for them to be beaten up? No more so than in Cheltenham.

Halfway through my stay, a guy named Geoff told me in a bar called the Beehive on the southern perimeter of the town centre how, many years ago, Cheltenham's pomposity began to spiral out of control when its councillors developed a passion for flowers. With this hitherto unheard-of new facility for winning the Britain in Bloom competition – due, he claimed, to a combination of the floral borders of the beer garden alongside the

Promenade and a substantial amount of bum action between the organisers and the council – its tourist office now advertises 'Guided walking tours of Regency Cheltenham' which are fronted by 'floral decorations'. Bourgeois creeps. ('No it *doesn't* – a Cheltonian.)

As with pubs in most of the rest of the country in the last ten years, drinking in the town is made an intimidating experience by the presence of bouncers on the entrances to many of the drinking establishments. Many of these date from the late 1980s when, as in much of the rest of the UK, a new brand of local catering business emerged in the town. Of course in Cheltenham these were as pretentious as anything. Red-brick buildings were erected, the cost being too great to travel as far as the Cotswolds to mine the less hideous limestone. These new places opened, adopting trendy names to appeal to school kids who had pocket money to blow, and changed hands as regularly as dreadful fashion stores did in the town centre in the early '70s when smaller non-chain outfits tried to compete in the same market as Chelsea Girl.

Meanwhile, as I write this chapter a debate is taking place over whether to build a multi-screen cinema complex and a further shopping arcade – this in a town which already has far more shops than it will ever need and an Odeon which only gets over-burdened with cinema-goers when a blockbuster is in town. Cheltenham seems very anxious to emulate Slough and Luton and every other nondescript English location. The combination of the locals' empty-headedness and the local councillors' corruption makes such a building programme inevitable. The future existence of these shabby emporia will stand as testimony to the fact that everyone in this particular town is bored out of his or her tiny mind. Bugger the consequences of a parade of tatty little shops which will spend their short lifetime changing hands before the whole structure's dismantled for a skating rink; we're bored.

In Cheltenham's case the debate circles around who is going to be behind this big development. Whitbread – which had recently taken over the local brewer Flowers – wants to use the site for a leisure complex including a ten-screen cinema complex with a few shops, while Waitrose wants to put in a supermarket. As a guy named Tom put it conservatively in the Promenade Vaults, a further ten cinema screens 'could be over-egging the pudding'.

Cheltenham's twentieth-century history has been shaped by a series of inept and corrupt councils which, as in most places throughout England, has resulted in meltdown. Its last Tory MP, Charles Irving, was a notorious pervert who managed to prevent his notoriety from becoming too public. Whether this arrogant queen was responsible for the influx of flowers, I do not know. But during his period as mayor of Cheltenham he was well known as a Cheltenham hotel owner (one of his premises was called Hotel Irving), and a primary purpose of the town's ever-increasing inflorescence was of course to attract visitors who would use the hotels.

Furthermore, although I don't have the details, commercial bribery will almost certainly have been central to the decision in the 1960s and 1970s to raze to the ground the town's remaining mediaeval buildings and to put in their place featureless concrete structures which then go through a lifetime of changed hands before they themselves are knocked down for shopping malls.

It is in keeping with Cheltenham's pretentiousness that the section of the High Street which was pedestrianised in the 1970s should be called The Strand and a 100-yard stretch of Montpellier should be called Little London. Until the last world war, its residents did indeed tend by and large to come from landed gentry or the upper levels of the armed forces. But not no more, matey. The Indian army's retreat, the New Club, was demolished some 30 years ago to make way for commercial expansion. About the only retired colonels in 'Nam nowadays are six feet underground.

A barman in a quiet pub off the town's Lower High Street kindly gave me a history lesson on the place. He told me how an influx of population from the north-east Midlands coming to work for such expanding companies as defence manufacturers Smiths and Dowty in their various factories around Cheltenham had swamped the town, filling up the pubs and riddling Cheltenham's traditional Gloucestershire accent with an ugliness normally found in circuses. I asked him for an example, and he said, 'The word "mum" is transformed into "merrm".' Nowadays the only survivors of this pre-industrial influx tend to be a working class which overwhelmingly aspires to middle class and fails, he said. This man was certainly not from Cheltenham. 'The town's population has mushroomed in the last couple of decades, and anyone with either talent or ambition has quit for London,' he said. I presume he meant both of them. But he's dead right – the modern Cheltenham accent is pretty unpleasant.

There is a surfeit of people who swan around town asking, 'Do you go down (*sic*) to London to do your shopping, or do you make do with Cavendish House?' They don't even pronounce it 'Hice'. And like you'd imagine the spoiled daughter of a vicar to say to impress her friends in her first year of higher education, a number of the local women will say incongruous things like, '*Definitely* the best in Cheltenham.' About anything. *Why?*

The fact remains that the majority of the population nowadays comprises those who pepper their conversations with speculation over how much such and such a local band, dedicated to writing anti-drugs songs or whatever, has made for the charity it has set up. A significant subset of these will also be including figures on how much is understood subsequently to have been spent on drugs. My friend the barman gestured to a group of these people in the far corner of the bar. Their leather gear dated from the early 1980s and it clung to them and seemed as though they slept in it.

Nearby Gloucestershire Airport in Staverton used to be notorious as an entry point for drugs, and one of the town's less unlikely claims to fame is that it was allegedly once considered to be the drugs capital of England.

And it has pretensions to becoming a city. 'Boots Corner is Cheltenham's answer to Sloane Square,' I was told by one local with the help of an interpreter. I rest my feet. Building development, meanwhile, has swallowed up many of the surrounding villages which, as they come under the domain of a variety of equally corrupt town and parish councils, find their inner charm has fallen victim to such bogus developments as homes for retired clergy or multi-media libraries, which themselves retire once their novelty has worn off.

The land, meanwhile, is spoilt forever. The developers have taken their profits, the parish councillors their bribes. In the nearby spoiled village of Prestbury, a mile or two north-east of the town, a large patch of grassland listed in the Domesday Book as a place for grazing cattle, next to the church dating back to the eighth century, became this century simply a grassy field with elm trees and a place for picnics, but since the 1980s has become home to an ugly assortment of new but decaying buildings.

How did this happen? This large field was bequeathed by its late owner in the 1960s as 'an amenity for the villagers of Prestbury'. Then, 20 years later, the parish council petitioned parishioners for objections to the erection of an estate of homes for retired clergy in the village. The village was in uproar, with the villagers themselves responding via petition and ordering the parish council to keep their hands off what didn't belong to them. Besides, these retired clergy didn't even *come* from the area. So the scheme was scrapped and the villagers forgot about it.

Some six months later, building began anyway. The parish council had allegedly put out another notice, but they must have done it by semaphore after dark because most would still have objected, not least to the fact that the surrounding narrow lanes could not accommodate any more traffic. 'I certainly never saw anything which said they might be appealing,' said the sad-looking retired farmer in the village who told me all this in the ancient Plough pub, located opposite the church. I had no reason to disbelieve him. I took a walk down the lane to look at the new buildings myself, and wondered how many other villages in the country had been destroyed by greedy parish councillors.

I know this has happened all over the country, and that it is destined to continue happening at an alarming rate for as long as government administrations deem it either voteworthy or financially advantageous to allow building on green-belt sites. But it doesn't do any harm to reflect on just why the decay is happening.

In the same village, I was to discover, plans are afoot to build more bogus homes. Prestbury will change from being a village, the edge of which lies in picturesque beauty at the foot of a hill, to being an extension of Cheltenham that will spill with ugly and presumably red brick up the hillside. Quite why, I'm not sure. There are a couple of ancient narrow lanes which will have to be widened and their surrounds destroyed if any houses are to be built on those fields. Houses along the lane which marks the northern edge of the village are now all going up for sale, and understandably so: the peace which prevailed in the village of Prestbury for over a thousand years is being shattered. And given the slimy way in which, I am reliably informed, previous building campaigns occurred, I very much doubt there is anything above board with this one.

In the Plough pub the elderly farmer asked me to listen for the church bells. I'd been there an hour and had heard none. 'Bloody gone'n muted 'em, haven't they?' he said. It may or may not have been true but would certainly be in keeping with the new styling of the place.

The vacuousness of those who run Cheltenham, making it in fact more the Centre for the Arse End of England than the Centre for the Cotswolds, spread to surrounding towns in the 1980s. Back in central Cheltenham in a pub called Tailor's, a guy named Chris, who worked for the locally based insurance company Eagle Star, told me that the county of Gloucestershire had made a bid 15 years earlier to become entitled 'Royal Gloucestershire'. 'This was principally on the basis that it contained Highgrove, some 30 miles south of Cheltenham, home of the Prince of Wales and his late wife,' he said. 'Somebody thankfully stepped in, but not before the wretched district council had persuaded everyone that that was what the county was going to be called.' There's quite a lot of evidence of repressed anger in Cheltenham.

Education in Cheltenham is a strange mix. It has its two famous public schools, the Ladies' College and the Boys' College, situated on two of the most attractive sites on the edge of the town centre. Chris had gone to the Boys' College, he told me.

The two schools' results couldn't be much more different. The Ladies' College continues to live up to its reputation for producing educated and well-spoken young ladies. The Boys' College, on the other hand, works on the basis that, while it is possible for academic pupils to excel, it is better to develop a boy's character than it is his intellect. Consequently it is close to the bottom of the exam-performance league of public schools, and has also had a considerable amount of publicity connected with pupils' drug-taking. 'You won't find a better example of that than me,' said Chris. 'I'm 30 in a month and I spend my working life answering the phone to enquiries about insurance claims.'

Of those pupils whose families come from Cheltenham, those who leave the sixth form at the Boys' College without A levels worth speaking of tend to stay in the town and set up business with capital provided by their parents, who are used to spending upwards of £10k on annual school fees. They dress swankily and together comprise a significant proportion of that small-town phenomenon, the big fish in the small pond. 'I'm not one of those,' Chris said defensively as two tossers in suits pushed past us to the bar making the distinctive Cheltenham speech-substitute noise, a cross between a yodel and a growl, which the barmaid translated as 'two pints of Stella, please'. There's something pitiful about people wearing suits in a small town like Cheltenham.

Indicating the two tossers, Chris said, 'They move in arrogant circles, too far down the food chain to recognise how it is only privilege that has spared them from the jaws of Mother Nature's selection process. They thrive on knowing people who will supply them with drugs, and after a session they will swan into a lunchtime bar talking of tennis clubs and expensive cars.

'So far you might consider them to be no different from the types of wankers you get in the stockbroking and banking sectors in the City. Think again. Where are these people spending their lives? A poxy little provincial town. They seldom visit London, of which they are afraid, although they brag that their dealer brings the stuff down from London. They have certainly never visited the theatre, except perhaps when they were on a school trip to Stratford some 30 miles away. And they drive Porsches. You notice Porsches a lot in places like Cheltenham, and each time you do you know you're not far from a wanker.' Full of opinion was Chris.

'These people usually end up being single for an inordinately large period of their lives, too. Their female counterparts' – he indicated two girls in their early twenties with navy blue lambswool sweaters hanging over their shoulders – 'are seldom attracted to the wankers.'

He explained that the sudden amalgamation of the local girls' and boys' grammar schools had resulted in a massive drop in the number of local schoolchildren entitled to a selective education. I reflected that if I had lived there, had been born ten years later than I was and had been prevented from attending a grammar school by the above reason, I expect I would now be considering no win–no fee legal action against the local authority for introducing a policy which would have made me attend a comprehensive school where I would have been beaten up daily by the illiterate inarticulate. And that's just the teachers. Of course, now there is a campaign to end selective education altogether – thoroughly in keeping with the rest of the destruction which is fast reducing the country to the status of a condemned septic tank.

Meanwhile, when the youths at these Cheltenham comprehensive schools are not beating each other up during the long months that lead up to their GCSEs – a taxing hour during which they must fit the right shapes into the right holes in order to gain their grade As (or A's, as they would presumably have been taught) – they are picking fights with those pupils they see wearing grammar-school uniform. This pastime escalated when the grammar schools combined in the south end of the town to be located bang in the middle of an area of council estate-serving comprehensives, according to Chris.

There are a couple of other fee-paying schools in the town besides the two colleges, Whitefriars and Dean Close. Chris told me the latter had refused admission to David Bowie's son Zowie Bowie in the early 1980s for fear he would encourage drug-taking among pupils. Drug-taking at a public school? Couldn't possibly happen.

Then there is a Catholic girls' school, the convent. 'Slappers, the lot of them,' said Chris, who claimed he would be heading off later to 'roger' one of them that very night.

In fact, to quote Tom Brown, writing in *The Erotic Review*, whose editor is a former Cheltenham Ladies' College girl, Cheltenham is 'noted for the number of its excellent schools for girls. At the snootiest of these, the uniform is a distinctly unflattering A-line tweed skirt, imaginatively described in the prospectus as "sage-green". The girls here are all six feet tall, and each has three feet of blonde hair, Oxbridge brains and a tremendous enthusiasm for "lac"s.

'At the other end of the scale is the Roman Catholic convent. The uniform here is navy blue, and the girls are all, needless to say, total slappers.

'Somewhere between the two is a grammar school of Eliza-bethan foundation and high academic standards, whose girls are neither slappers nor exactly ladies. Their uniform is a scarlet lambswool sweater and a grey skirt, by design intended to reach to the knee but worn by many of the girls so as to resemble little more than a generous cummerbund.'

Cheltenham is deceptive. It isn't yet physically quite as ugly as Gloucester, although it's trying hard to get there by blotting out any attractive spots with hideous new buildings. But I have to put it at the top of the list of dreadful places to visit because it is a poxy little town with airs about itself which are as bogus as the new houses it builds at the expense of surrounding ancient fields and woodland. It is a perfect place for illustrating the logic behind the ruling party and its passion for destroying the livelihoods of farmers: it means they are more likely to sell up their farms, thus freeing up the land to be built upon by the party's greatest fundraisers, the building consortia. Just a thought. Not like it's damaging or anything, of course.

Apart from Chris, the barman and the retired farmer, I met absolutely nobody else the whole time I was there who had much to say apart from 'oo arr'. Flared trousers may be fashionable in Southport, nose studs in Brighton, but among the young people of Cheltenham the fashion is unwashed.

On my last night there I was exploring a nightclub close to the Promenade when, standing in a tweed jacket and trying to read the street sign, I looked up to the sound of a slurred high-pitched whistle. A bloke in 1970s outdoor wear caught my glance, lowered his head in a pseudo-inquisitive manner and said 'Oi!', and then, in a lower tone but with a distinctly West Country farming/Cheltenham estate agent accent, said 'Merchant wanker!' before heading back off into the night. Essentially, a voluntary trip to Cheltenham is not something I would recommend.

21. Stoke-on-Trent

No sense of humour and the nightlife is shit
– unless you're a prostitute

According to the woman who co-ran the bed and breakfast in Stoke-on-Trent, the city is the fifth most popular destination in England. This staggered me. Oh yes, she said, all due to the Potteries, and the new cultural centre. I was not violently aware of the existence of either before I arrived there. However, the woman in the tourist office wasn't sure how to go about disabusing me of this figure when I checked it with her. She hesitated, then said slowly, 'I'm not sure that it's *that* popular, though I haven't got the actual figures.'

A friend who used to work in Stoke summed up the Potteries in his own words. 'Your average Potteries resident is similar to a Scouser in many ways, in that they will rob you and they don't seem to mind living in a dump, but the big difference is they don't have a sense of humour and the nightlife is shit.'

But I'd never had such a welcome in a bed and breakfast. As soon as I had rung the bell the landlady opened the door, welcomed me with a warm smile and reassured me I could stay for £24, which wasn't bad, and was a tenner less than I'd paid to stay the night in Gloucester.

She proudly showed me a city guide she had compiled herself, a copy of which she left in each bedroom. It described in detail everything from restaurants and nightclubs to the sightseeing attraction, the Potteries. Entertainment comprised a ski centre, Water World (was this a division of Stoke-based Armitage Shanks, I wondered), Superbowl and a ten-screen cinema complex.

I explained the purpose of my visit. 'Do you hear that, Edith? Gentleman's writing a book on travel and he's including Stoke-on-Trent,' she exclaimed. Edith had come in to offer me a cup of tea prior to my ordeal.

In addition the place now included a Royal Theatre, Victoria Hall for concerts, and an art gallery. All had been developed in about the last year, courtesy of the local council, which had allegedly wanted to clean up the image of the city. That or make a fat pile of cash out of developers and stay in power – it's a tricky one. Curiously, nobody had anything to say in the city centre about what proportion of the profits made from its enterprises was being channelled out to the surrounding massive and massively depressed council estates. 'Oh yes, there are some bad places here. But the council's pumped loads of money into the cultural centre,' said the landlady. So *that's* all right then.

I set off for the centre of Hanley, the capital of the five or so municipalities which make up the city of Stoke-on-Trent. Here starvation was not as much of a threat to me as it had been in Gloucester. There was no shortage of pubs and most of these provided lunch at non-London prices. I managed to have scampi and chips with a pint for under a fiver.

But where Stoke is tidying itself up, it's going the only way anywhere in this country seems to know how: the sanitised route. For instance, a monstrous JD Wetherspoons pub dominated the horizon approaching the main shopping centre, with all its new-age social bullshit and rules which eliminate any personality, individual freedom or imagination: 'Remember your table number at the bar', 'You cannot smoke in this section', etc. All very American.

And it has enabled further hardwood-furnished pub chains to embed themselves in the psyche of the English pleb. The Pig and Truffle could be any other theme pub like the Slug and Lettuce, the only difference being that instead of music for the thirty-somethings playing, the voice of a camp New Zealander could be heard introducing track after track of rap music for the under-14s. At least they each knew their target audience, I suppose.

A poster lodged between the clearly fake 'memorabilia' boasted that the pub's events were 'sponsored by Carlsberg –

Ask at the bar for any promotional details'. Are they *serious*? Clearly there had been some transformation in the social fabric of the nation that I had missed. I asked for a box of matches at the bar and when I was handed back my change I was instructed to have a nice day. However, listening to 40-decibel radio adverts was not my idea of being entertained, so I didn't stay for a drink.

Yates' Wine Lodge, bang next door, was almost exactly the same, as though owned by the same consortium but dressed up *very slightly* differently, the main difference being the tone of wood varnish, to fool a gullible public. It's a tragedy to think that these places are successful.

Facing these bars in a short, off-the-high-street cul-de-sac was Trinity's, yet another one based on the same fraudulent basis of hardwood and fake nostalgic signs. But this one had cushions – amazing the difference these made. The spuriousness of the signs purporting to be antique was immediately given away by the habit encouraged by post-'60s teachers of liberally misusing apostrophes. I mean apostrophe's. One of them advertised cigarette's.

The effects, however bad, seemed to be bringing in the tourists, though. It was Monday morning and there was a queue in the tourist office, which clearly saw a lot more action than its Gloucester counterpart.

Many of the older established pubs in Stoke share the same features: they are poorly lit Victorian establishments, and most seem to have acquired their door styles from the same supplier. A surprisingly high proportion of the local pubs have black doors leading through to the toilets, where another local Stoke supplier, Armitage Shanks, has furnished their smallest rooms' interiors.

I took a glance at the local evening paper that day, the *Stoke Sentinel*, dateline 10 May 1999: FOREIGN OFFICE ADVISES BRITONS TO STAY OUT OF CHINA. And the opening sentence? 'Business people *in Staffordshire* [my italics] were today warned . . .' To be fair, which I'm not, the Potteries had recently opened negotiations with China, which itself had

167

not long opened its borders to trade with the West. But you sure as hell knew from the style of the local rag that you were out of London and amidst people with very different horizons. And the *Sentinel* still preached to low ambition like any other local paper outside London or Scotland, dedicating columns to desperately trivial affairs or achievements.

This all reassured me that modern provincial life, and the compromises it makes, have resulted in the setting of standards among a population which didn't even blink when a free Staffordshire weekly paper printed a letter from a concerned mother:

> Sir,
>
> The other day I was horrified to see a small boy wearing a sweatshirt with the words I WISH I WERE BIGGER.
>
> Its (*sic*) bad enough children having to watch violence on TV without clothing manufacturers teaching them bad grammar . . .

I thought I'd take a more detailed look around Stoke to see what its cluster of towns was like.

The round trip by bus from Hanley to Meir went via Bentilee and Weston Coney. Bentilee and Meir were complete and utter dumps. Many of the houses were boarded up, and young kids were running around in what resembled a scene from a Third World countryii.

The sad bastards that must suffer most are those people who purchased their own property and are now trapped, living in a crime-ridden shithole and owning a house that has no value. And due to the fact that their properties have double glazing and a well-kept garden, they are considered a legitimate target for the local scumbags.

The recent extension to the A50 into south Stoke has apparently improved things considerably by knocking down large areas and turning them into a dual carriageway – at the same time dividing the community even further. Weston Coney is meant to be the posh end of south Stoke, but it is still a complete dump.

By night I only got to see Hanley, whose streets fill with prostitutes at around sunset. Christ knows what the surrounding estates are like at night. I sensed I was in what must have been the origin of Essex-girl jokes. How can you tell that a girl from Longton is having an orgasm? She drops her chips.

Say what you like about Stoke – and there is much to say that *is* bad about the place, especially about the terror that grips you as you travel through the suburbs and the highly populated but neglected housing estates – but there appears to be a great deal more optimism in the public at large than in centres further south which have equally little reason to feel it. This, I concluded, was where a parallel could be drawn between the residents of Stoke and those of Liverpool.

I had immediately sensed that I was passing through the gateway to the north as I witnessed people more openly polite and less guarded than their counterparts closer to London. Bar staff all seemed eager to satisfy their customers, and the contempt I'd been shown in Gloucester was nowhere to be seen. Friendliness rather than aggression prevailed in the public bars. (I have to say, though, that the beer was all of noticeably poorer quality in Hanley than in London, so I clearly wasn't in the real north if its own tedious claims are anything to go by.)

There isn't even the sense that prevails in other provincial centres – that life begins and ends there. Even Hanley's only *Big Issue* salesman said he commuted south daily from Manchester. The local mixture of accents suggested the population was anything but static.

I went to bed puzzled that night. Was Stoke really not that bad after all? In order to put my mind at ease and reassure myself that life really was anything *but* beautiful in Stoke-on-Trent, the next morning I went into a sister shop of a high street electrical appliance outlet to collect the latest version of its free Internet CD. I wanted to know that at least in shops where you expect poor service, you get it. And, sure enough, I did. 'We don't have any,' said the assistant in a tone that was anything but keen.

'Then can you tell me of anywhere else that may have them in Stoke?' I asked.

'Nowhere round here,' came the reply. But 100 yards deeper into the shopping arcade I entered another shop of the same chain which had 'hundreds of the things' and whose assistant happily handed one to me. I guess it's the same everywhere nowadays: anyone in menial work is unburdened by a sense of duty and untrained by management to serve the general public.

My initial reaction to Stoke-on-Trent had been that the efforts by the local council, however cynical these were, and in spite of the hundreds of posters on street corners displaying the picture of a smug local councillor and advertising her efforts, had helped improve greatly on what I understand was there not long before my visit. However, after seeing the surrounding estates I realised that change was hardly going to be of benefit to the vast majority of the population. The sum total of achievement is that it is now possible to pop into Hanley's centre by day and *feel* relatively safe.

I also began to see that what I had expected was taking rather a different form: towns north of Gloucestershire seemed to *lack* that particular county's most prominent feature of oafish philistines bidding inarticulately and in vulgar accents to be the most important man in town.

Overall there was only a scattering of retardates, Staffordshire's villages clearly not being the havens for incest that their counterparts are in rural Gloucestershire and East Anglia. And there seemed to be noticeably fewer teenage arcade rats hanging around together and sharing the hopelessness of their existence. Yet youth, I noticed, tended to be a great deal more spotty and obese than in London. From a fashion perspective, there were fewer tracksuits but more cloth caps in north Staffordshire. It was an odd place to be.

I was impressed by the willingness of locals to help. I asked a Sikh running a stall in an indoor market if he could tell me where Glass Street was. In a broad Scouse accent he kindly volunteered to draw me a map of how to get there – once I'd been able to understand that his miscomprehension of my question was simply down to the fact that I had been pronouncing 'Glass' with a southern 'ah'.

The bar staff in Stoke's Firkin pub were more civilised and less pretentious than those in others I'd seen in London, the first port of call for the sterile concept of new-age service and where it was first piloted before being rolled out to the rest of England. I hoped it was symptomatic of the area, though it might have been because the bar was an exception and, instead of brewing the beer on its premises, the kegs were brought up from Stafford some 20 miles away.

It may also be that pub landlords have little choice, but the pubs themselves displayed less inclination to throw out reprobates than those in Gloucester, suggesting a broader-minded approach to business with less fear of anything that didn't match the narrow standards it set. This complacency seemed to have had the effect of producing a more intense sense of paranoia among visitors. Certainly in me.

But that was Stoke in the daytime, where, after a day in Gloucester, it was harder than I had expected to say anything negative about the place. When night fell, however, the veil fell with it.

Earlier in the day I had concluded that the people of Stoke seemed to have what was lacking in places further south such as Gloucester and Swindon: a sense of humour, albeit vague. However, as the average age of people in Hanley centre fell 60 per cent to around 21 at about 7 p.m., I was confronted by a population that worried me deeply.

In an area close to Hanley's centre, where every building is a theme pub and most likely owned by one business consortium, I was sitting reading about factory tours in *A Visitor's Guide to Stoke-on-Trent* when I was offered a drink by a pair of first-year students, Johnny and Mark. Johnny was celebrating his 18th birthday. It was happy hour on what is known in Stoke as Student Night and to the rest of the English-speaking world as Monday.

I declined the kind offer, as I had just bought a whisky, and besides, I couldn't take money from students when Nice Tony was making their lives more expensive than ever. But, uninvited, they came over and joined me. 'It's Johnny's birthday,' I was told.

They asked what I was doing and I told them.

'It's rough in Stoke, very rough,' said Mark.

'Rough as fuck,' said Johnny. 'Prostitutes,' he added as though by way of explanation.

I asked what they did for a living. 'We're students at the University of Manchester, which is in Stoke,' said Mark, who explained that he was doing a degree in PE and that Johnny was doing a degree in *teaching* PE. Beyond that they had no answers to anything I asked. I could not bring them to be interesting on the subject of anything that would be worthy of inclusion in the book. I tried to find out more about the dangers to which Johnny had eluded, but all I got back was, 'It's not dangerous like London.' I tried to find their reasoning for this when as far as I had concluded the rate of crime per capita in Stoke sounded a lot worse than London. But he insisted, 'My dad lives there. He says there's *lots* of prostitutes in London.' Well, if Johnny was training to be a teacher then he was nearly there if he wanted to match current standards.

I crashed out on the bed when I arrived back in the B&B but was woken half an hour or so later by voices from the next room, the walls of the guest house being made of cardboard. I heard every word spoken by four guys from Manchester who had finished their shift and were drinking cans of Carlsberg and Heineken and eating takeaway curry. This went on till about 5 a.m. So I was very tired when I left Stoke.

22. Derby

Decay dressed up as modernisation

In spite of my fatigue, on arrival in Derby I found it initially to be an arrestingly pleasant place. For a start it wasn't Cheltenham. The local accent varied but was by and large inoffensive, which is more than can be said for Gloucester or, as Beryl Bainbridge so rightly points out, Liverpool. And there was no local council policy of advertising invisible achievements on every street corner. But it suddenly lost all credibility when I read in the Derby tourist brochure, 'As one of the great British cities . . .' That's like the former Slough College of Higher Education describing itself as 'one of the great universities'.

Derby was, as far as I could see, an anonymous place, and at first glance was so inoffensive that I had to resort to using the local municipal library from which to launch my study of the place. A book which could have related to virtually any town in England, *Yesterday's Town* by John Heath and Ray Christianson, begins with an unattributed quote of 1887, that 'most towns, as they grow older, become newer, for the aged buildings are cleared off and young ones take their place, and to no place does this observation more closely apply than Derby. Could people return who have not seen Derby for the last 15 or 20 years, they would not recognise the place, so startling has been the change.'

The town became a city in 1977 when, in a moment of profound insanity during her Jubilee year, the Queen granted it the (ir)relevant Royal Charter – something to which all pretentious town councils aspire, not least Cheltenham. Poor, hapless twits.

The town – sorry, city – of Derby itself has been avoided by most of the folk of what has become Derbyshire for the whole of the last millennium; this book by Heath and Christianson reckons the first Derby bypass was built in AD 800.

When you compare that book, heavily illustrated as it is with turn-of-the-century photographs, and present-day Derby, you see there has been little change to the look of the place in the last 100 years. There has been far more change in Cheltenham in the past 30 years. Derby architecture still looks how it has done since the nineteenth century: industrial. And if there is any truth in Balzac's claim that one's face is a reflection of one's surroundings, it explains Derby citizens' lack of a need for self-deception.

Derbyans look somehow different from southerners. There seems to be an abundance of plump, rosy-cheeked landladies (or landlady's, as any 1990s state secondary-school teacher would explain) for a start. The endearing and affectionate northern lilt was beginning to come through loud and clear.

Armed with this major insight into Derby I headed through the wet streets to the tourist office, where my status as a serious travel writer was rewarded with a *free* copy of the Derby 1999 visitor's guide – saving me 30 pence.

The place has a couple of mediaeval buildings and it's in the Peak District. But city as it may now claim to be, it still shares most of the features of other small provincial towns. It has the curious but mandatory one-way traffic schemes, and a population obsessed with shopping, largely because there's bugger all else to do. And its architects of the last 20 years appear to have had as little imagination as the rest of them. The tourist guide begins, 'Shopping in Derby's pedestrianised city centre promises . . . ,' (yawn) and continues, 'Today's high-street names bring shopping right up to date in the modern shopping areas with a huge range of shops under one roof . . . the Audley Centre and the Main Centre, where you will find the crafters' Market Place featuring over 400 stalls of handmade or hand-finished products.' The English disease, decay, dressed up as modernisation.

So on to the pubs. Bar meals were beginning to become restricted, and an indication that I was heading north was that mushy peas came with everything. Even the soup.

The centre of the city has 'family local' pubs which, as in the provinces further south, include thirty-something biker bachelors seeking a role in life and embalming themselves and their leather jackets in clichés, ritual laughter and gossip. With them are their leather-clad ex-girlfriends rocking prams containing their leather-clad infants.

One boring tit standing by the bar seemed to have only the one role in life, which was to be on first-name terms with the bar staff. The landlady had dark hair styled in the fashion of the children's cartoon character Crystaltips, and she wore tight ripped jeans and trainers. Heavy metal logos were stuck to the optics behind her. Deep Purple played on the jukebox, and a scruffy, balding, middle-aged guy in a mixed suit was slouched on a chair with a glass still in his hand. Perhaps he'd died. I didn't stay long enough to find out.

The walls of the bar were decorated with framed black-and-white photographs which had presumably been issued by the brewery. The most prominent of these had had its glass broken and photo removed and a small poster of a motorcycle racer in transit leaning into a bend had been Blu-Tacked in its place. Wow. Rebellion.

The Old Silk Mill, a nearby pub and hotel, smelled less of dirty laundry, so I ordered a full pint. As I had approached the inn, which overlooked a church on one side and a multi-storey car park on the other, I had heard more skilfully applied church bell-ringing than I could recall ever having heard. But it had started to rain again, so into the pub I went.

No, it didn't smell as bad, but it might as well have done, for although there were a few suits chatting to the landlord, there was a high number of undesirables: unwashed white Rastafarian talking to black Rastafarian – it was, of course, difficult to tell if the latter had washed. To anyone accusing me of skirting on historical significance, I say again: I *see* no historical significance, as seldom is the history reflected in the living inhabitants in these places.

Derby seems to have a population more in transit than you get further south, with an amalgamation of Scouse, Mancunian and Yorkshire accents. I noted this as I dragged my suitcase through the cobbled streets to find a bed and breakfast – just as I noticed I really was getting into trousers-with-ironed-creases country.

Some 15 years earlier, *Punch* magazine, under the editorial control of Alan Coren, received just one response worth printing following its competition to write a humorous picture caption. This followed the publication earlier in the year of a student supplement, and the picture, to give whoever sent in the winning caption his due, was of a youth standing before a ticket booth, wearing an over-filled rucksack with various pans and sleeping bags tied to the side. The winning quote was, 'Platform ticket, please.' Coren wrote an accompanying editorial with the line to the effect that university wit was now dead. Well, if the early 1980s produced one response worth printing, 1999 would sure as hell result in none. That is unless the fashionable, uncompetitive practice of cheating, so widely taught in schools these days, was used, such as employing someone at least in his mid-thirties to make up the caption.

But it's nearly the end of the current millennium and it's an accepted fact that students are a universally talentless and unimaginative bunch of boring gits – just one aspect of English decay. Asked if he could suggest any good pubs, the B&B proprietor sighed and said, 'This is a university city so there are a lot of theme pubs in the centre, I'm afraid.' Need I say more?

It was uncanny but soon after I'd embarked on my subsequent trawl through Derby's pubs I overheard a middle-aged businessman ask, 'Is this music meant to clear the pub and give you maximum breathing space?' It's ironic that the '60s rebels like him are now saying what they themselves used to generate: the 'not *this*!' reaction.

But scattered around the square mile that is Derby – not that that should count against its alleged entitlement to the status of city since, let's face it, the City of London is known as the Square Mile – there are a few unspoilt pubs. One of these dates from the 1530s, Ye Old Dolphine Inne, which is not listed in Derby Council's tourist guide and which upstairs has a most spectacular restaurant up a seemingly original narrow wooden stairway. I followed the barmaid, who, to make up for her lack of historical knowledge of the building, offered to get the keys to unlock the restaurant and show me the dining-room. I banged my head twice as I walked behind her – proof perhaps that this place really was built in a time when people were shorter than they are today. Nowadays only children, or adults of the diminutive stature of Tom Cruise, could sprint safely up to that restaurant.

No one working in the pub had any idea of its history when I asked for further detail than was provided on the plaque on the building's front. In the pub itself, at 2.45 p.m., a conversation was being conducted beside the bar by a retired bloke in his fifties and addressed at two other locals, one in a suit preparing to return to work and another with clearly no work to which to return.

The retired bloke had an air of having made it in life, which was rather sad as he was whiling away his afternoons talking to the only people who would listen. Most of his conversation centred around how pathetic he considered other patrons of the bar to be for not knowing their ales or their wine. He mentioned a French vintage and *recommended* it, so his intelligence was suspect.

I ambled down the road to the Vaults – 'said to be the only ones in Derby', according to the tourist literature. Well, surely if anyone else owned vaults there they would have been quick to point out the error. The Vaults were on a 'city' centre high street with the usual town shops, but all the shops were in their original nineteenth-century brick buildings, which was pleasant and interesting to see – unlike everywhere else I'd so far encountered outside London.

And the Vaults were a Vivian Stanshallesque place to get a free pint. A television screen above the bar displayed activity on the stone stairway outside the bar which led down from street level to the vaults themselves. One could get an acquaintance to distract the bar staff while one put a blood-soaked dummy on the stairs and came into the bar. On seeing him, the other could look horrified at the screen. The barman would rush out and in his absence oneself and one's acquaintance could fill their glasses from the unattended bar. Sadly, I was travelling alone.

I drank the pint for which I'd had to pay and left to walk again along the attractive high street – about the only attractive provincial street in England. It might have been the aesthetically pleasing nature of the buildings themselves that caused me to look in the window of an estate agent and discover the first and probably only interesting thing about non-London England: house prices. Suddenly, after months spent cumulatively out of London, I had found something in which it was possible to become mentally absorbed. As the joint owner of a mortgage on a London flat, I was spellbound. Property was about one quarter the price. They didn't even *sell* flats as small as ours, which I had acquired for a tad under £100,000 earlier that year.

I entered the estate agent's premises and saw that £30,000 would buy me a house in central Derby with three bedrooms, two receptions, a loft conversion and a garden. I even had to stop and think. I didn't wish to dwell on that thought, not least because I had fallen upon a place which I did not even begin to hate during my stay there. Not after Gloucester. Certainly not after Cheltenham. And Derby had only been an accidental discovery: taking that particular route was to make my train fare on to Sheffield even cheaper.

But, like all the rest of the places I visited, it was a little population centre, with its own little cultural idiosyncrasies, none of which has great significance. In the words of the B&B landlady, 'The ring road is *crap*.' The landlord added, 'Derby is dwarfed by its neighbour Nottingham, 15 miles away. Everything in terms of traffic or weather relates to there.' So maybe that is why it is so unspoiled; maybe I was witnessing the fruits of those who decided to build the first bypass in the eighth century.

And bouncers were only on the pubs' doors at the weekend.

Oh, I *see* now – I hadn't even bothered to mention it, but Derby City Council's logo is 'Derby*es*', with the 'es' in the same colour but *slightly* italicised. Vaguely around the last three letters is a rather careless speech bubble, and beneath it are the words 'the city where you can . . .'. I must have looked at that a hundred times before working out what it means. I think it means to spell 'yes' – a very clever use of the last letter to spell a word that clearly sums up Derby. I'd assumed the 'e' and the 's' stood for something like Enterprise Scheme, dreamt up by someone on community service, or a YTS.

23. Sheffield

Vandalism, drug-taking and teenage pregnancy
are a way of life

I wanted to escape. This was, I had thought, a big northern city, yet it appeared to have exactly the same local town planners as the rest of the English nightmare.

I walked out of the station and passed a newsagent's selling the *Sheffield Star*. Its headline read 'City burglars "addicted to heroin"'. Wow – first with the news up here. Then you step deeper into the surroundings of concrete and Mr Buy Rite and Dixons and red tiles and unhelpful pedestrian signs to City Hall and to this shopping centre or that one. Wherever I wanted to go I was abandoned to guesswork.

The next thing I noticed was Yates' Wine Lodge with its mass of rainforest wood furnishings and where, inside, it was impossible to escape the volume of the powerful loudspeakers pumping out teenage favourites of the moment. Nice stereo; shame about the music.

It was then that I finally succumbed to purchasing a portable CD player. Sheffield somehow managed to do that to me. For the best part of 15 years I had happily lived with compact cassettes and vinyl LPs, secure in the knowledge that CDs were 13 times the cost of second-hand LPs and that the fragile little things are so clinically reproduced that the sound, especially on classical records, is nothing compared to the sound of a vintage analogue pressing. CDs were also widely acknowledged to be a complete rip-off for never having anything on the B-side. Yet here I was walking out of a Dixons of all places with a CD player. It didn't even come with a sample CD. My ITT compact cassette recorder had in 1974 at least come with a free 30-minute pre-recorded 'light music' tape.

So I had to go to a CD store to find out what it sounded like.

Bloody useless waste of space that purchase was, I was to discover. 'Portable' it called itself. Move the thing and the music bounced around worse than a turntable in an earthquake.

So all of a sudden I was the proud owner of post-1984 music technology. My hopes, which hadn't been high, weren't subsequently dashed by the discovery that the player kept sticking and stopping. And it sounded like a distant loudspeaker playing against the invasive noise of what was mostly commercials when I was back in another pub whose decor came from some rainforest or other.

Anyway, I sat in the 'pub' and read the city council's tourist bumph, trying to listen through headphones to *The Sound of Bread*. Sheffield's council failed to list any pubs at all in its 66-page 'In and Around Sheffield' guide. It just listed cafés such as the so-called US-style Henry's, but when I was eventually to meet up with an old friend who lived a couple of miles north of the city, I was actually to find pubs galore. But in the city centre it's all theme places with blackboards with such suicide-inducing slogans as 'millennium meal deal'. A bloke serving in one pub explained that bars suffered in Sheffield through the frequent closure of nightclubs. 'Used to be one just across the road. That closed a couple of weeks back. We'll be next.'

I finished my pint and made my way on through the rain to the library.

Sheffield is the fourth largest city in England with a population estimated in 1991 to be over 500,000, but its 12-year-old girls are known to have been working hard to raise that, so a decade on the total is probably a lot higher.

The city is close to the M1, M62 and M18 motorways. Its nearest city neighbours are Leeds in West Yorkshire and Manchester in Lancashire. It's also close to Barnsley. And when Dougal landed on the moon with the blue cat in the 1973 film *Dougal and the Blue Cat*, he sighed, 'What a place – it's worse than Barnsley.' However, I had no time to visit the place myself. I trust Dougal implicitly.

Time was in the early 1980s when the Sheffield Students'

Union would boycott any of its members caught in possession of a Barclaycard or who spared a thought for the Tory party, or so I had been told by school acquaintances who had taken up their education there. I was disgusted then, but now there isn't any evidence of the slightest trace of reaction from the local student population. They've joined the nationwide meltdown and are more interested in what the next episode of *Neighbours* has in store than in the fact that most members of the current ruling party that had just engaged in war in Kosovo had some 15 years earlier been sitting in the rain promoting lesbianism at Greenham Common and pronouncing school playgrounds nuclear-free zones. Their contemporaries can now all be found employed in state secondary schools.

Sheffield is a big place with its quota of boarded-up homes. For large residential areas of the city, vandalism, drug-taking and teenage pregnancy are a way of life. Its housing estates are home to tens of thousands of teenage burglars. A column in London's *Evening Standard* quoted a girl who had lived on one such estate: 'I lived here for five years, and I was always getting burgled. It's not really a working-class area – nobody seems to work.'

The part of the city where one first arrives in Sheffield, the part the tourists get to see and where the councillors line their wallets, is the city centre, where an astronomically large amount of money has been spent disguising the fact that nearby are some of the most violent Western population spots outside the US.

But I would hate to be unfair to anywhere I cite in this book by concentrating on something I have witnessed without balancing my view with the rest of the municipality's surrounding area. As I wandered back into the centre of the city to get a train on to Harrogate, I was just thinking that, given the short amount of time I had left there, I couldn't write up Sheffield in the same detail in which I had done the other places in this book, when I was mugged.

I was coming down a hillside, a little pissed, a spring sunset ahead of me colouring the otherwise grey and unattractive city, when this dim 14-year-old Yorkshire voice came out at me from a side alley off the street: 'Joost give us your moonny.' I didn't hesitate – I only had £20 on me. The horrible little child had syringe marks on his forearms, I noticed, as he turned and scarpered. I shouted angrily after him, 'Shouldn't you be at school?' Would it have helped if I'd told the police? Was I really neglecting my duty as the only responsible citizen in Sheffield that day? I'll leave that up to you to work out.

So I take back anything pleasant I might accidentally have said about the place. It stinks. I've lived in east London for ten years and never been mugged (apart from when I lived in Forest Gate and was mugged three times in the space of a week). I'd spent just two days in Sheffield and I was shitting myself.

24. Harrogate

'If Harrogate ever had life, it was dead now'
– adapted quote from Withnail and I

A bit stuck out of the way is Harrogate.

I found myself travelling from Leeds on a two-carriage train, through the rich Yorkshire countryside, on the approach to Harrogate. As I neared my destination there was a break in the clouds and I could see what appeared to be a charming country town looming ahead of us.

I stepped from the station into the quiet centre of the town which had clearly seen a great deal of pseudo-classical style work carried out on its shop fronts in recent years. It had the 1990s style of pedestrian paving which will be in fashion in Harrogate and any number of other twee English towns for at least the next three years and which involves less loud drilling and more quiet lifting of slabs whenever the utilities are in town than conventional tarmac.

But, of course, life isn't always that straightforward. Near the flower market in Bethnal Green a few years ago, Tower Hamlets council overhauled a ten-yard stretch of Wellington Row as part of a traffic-calming scheme. Workmen seemed to take weeks laying the slabs in an elaborate pattern. Two days after they finished, one privatised utility turned up and spent the day drilling through the tiles. When they had finished, one quarter of the patterned slabs was replaced with tarmac. The council thoughtfully reinstated the patterned slabs a few weeks later, but it did seem an awful waste of my council tax bill.

Anyway, I needed a pub in which to quench my thirst and from which to call the friends at whose house I would be staying that night. By this stage in the journey my suitcase weighed so much that even on wheels it was a heavy burden, thanks to the books and other memorabilia I had acquired on my travels.

There was no pub to be seen from the railway station in the town centre. I had three choices: to turn left or right, or to follow a road the far side of an elaborate pedestrian crossing. I chose the last and headed for a board a hundred yards further on which I hoped would suggest a drink. The surrounding population appeared to have been of an age which preceded the original introduction of licensing laws.

Sure enough, the sign did denote the serving of alcohol, but the place itself was as themed as they come, with more hardwood than I'd seen since the clean pub district in Stoke-on-Trent. As I approached it I was confronted by three superannuated, furrowed-browed, white-hat-clad women and an older man shuffling along sans haste and with no apparent intention of making way for me and my suitcase. I stepped on to the pavement and heard one of them – probably the man, though I couldn't be certain – muttering something in German. It reminded me of Madeira, where my wife and I had spent our honeymoon earlier that year and where I had experienced an uncanny sense that I was unlikely ever again to be surrounded by such a rich collection of Nazi war criminals.

To be fair, I think one of the Harrogate passers-by was Italian. She was sporting a grand dark moustache which spread in waves beneath the leaning tower of her nose.

Harrogate did, I noticed, possess qualities absent in most of the provincial centres further south: it is far enough away from anywhere to bother trying to pretend it is anything other than what it is, a little Yorkshire town. How much less polluted the highways of England would be, how much fresher the air, if only Cheltenham, for instance, accepted that it is a little Gloucestershire town with a high crime rate midway between Birmingham and Bristol, rather than London in the centre of the Cotswolds.

My initial optimism at Harrogate, however, was knocked for six when it dawned on me that all the sad qualities of towns further south were simply in the early stages of migration. One day they'll reach Scotland, and then civilisation will be at an end. In the same way that every other manifestation of America's greatest export, social problems, makes its way over here (obsessive litigation, gun crime, *The Jerry Springer Show*, etc.), so the so-called dumbing down of Britain is marching irreversibly towards Carlisle and beyond.

I went into a theme pub whose name I forget but which appeared to have been named by some twenty-something post-graduate who had not so much read as looked at the pictures of his specialist subject, to find a spotty youth in stripy uniform (green or blue – I'm colour-blind) standing behind the bar. He hadn't even had to be told to avoid displaying a sense of humour – he was born without one. I asked if there was a payphone, and he gestured to the other side of the bar.

Returning to the modern Neanderthal, who happened to be wearing an ironed shirt, I made the mistake of trying to indulge in light-hearted banter with him. I told him of the time when, working in a local village pub in Surrey ten years earlier, I had been approached by a stranger who walked in, thrust a florin at me and said, 'Call me a taxi!' I then told the young barman that I had replied swiftly to that with, 'You're a taxi!'

The wrinkled gaze of my interlocutor in Harrogate indicated I suppose that he was at least *trying* to work out what the point of the story was. I retreated and sat down at a table, next to one at which was seated a teenage school-leaver of around 17 or 18 stone who had the facial complexion of a deep-pan pizza. On the table before him was an Airfix model he was attempting to assemble, or at least whose instructions he was studying. Ten minutes later I left. He hadn't shifted his gaze from the sheet of unfolded instructions.

I caught a cab round the corner and met my friend James and his wife Jenni. I remarked on some of my findings in Harrogate which would qualify it to feature in this study of England's sit-upon, and he explained that they had once had the misfortune to live and work in Stoke-on-Trent and therefore anything negative I was to say about Harrogate would fall on deaf ears.

So we went to find a pub. James proceeded to tell me, as we passed a newspaper stall selling what looked like the *Harrogate Times*, that Harrogate is the stag-party centre of Yorkshire. 'They flock here in droves from Leeds, York, Sheffield and even Hull,' he said.

In spite of Yorkshire's reputation for tight-fisted locals – it has been said that Yorkshiremen descend from those Scots who, on marching to London a few hundred years ago, were too mean to finish the journey – I encountered a surprising level of willingness from strangers to help out wherever I went. Perhaps it was just that by this stage of my journey I was so bewildered by the different provinces.

To (mis)quote Marwood in *Withnail and I*, if Harrogate ever had life, it was dead now. Essentially, while Harrogate is great to look at, the once-traditional values of the people of the county of Yorkshire have vanished to be replaced by zombies whose personalities are as vacant as those you might find anywhere else.

At Harrogate's railway station the next day, the almost Italian eagerness to appear helpful extended a little further than I needed it to. I'd just turned up for the trip back to London and expected a long wait. But the woman behind what had once been a British Rail counter smiled, said that would be £42 and that the train would be leaving from platform one in four minutes. I was delighted.

Of course, it was half an hour late, but that was largely the fault of the guard on the three-carriage vehicle whose job it was to inspect tickets and to operate the train's doors. He seemed to be past the age of retirement and certainly wasn't risking his ageing limbs by hurrying over anything.

There were a dozen or so stops between Harrogate and York, and each time the train stopped at a station the guard would be at the other end of the train from the door controls, inspecting tickets. Making about as much haste as the butler in *Camberwick Green* answering the phone, he would spend much of the day returning the length of the train, whereupon he would double-check that we had stopped, open the doors, then walk across the platform, where he would stand waiting for God knows what as the last passengers to have disembarked became smaller and smaller dots on the horizon. Then he would climb on board again, pause and finally close the doors. This process must have added 40 minutes or so to each journey to and from Harrogate.

When he came to inspect my ticket, he told me it was invalid. Only an hour before I'd specifically asked for a ticket on the next train to London via York, I said.

'Well, this is a supersaver.'

I didn't care what it was called. I had specified and bought a ticket, so I should not have to pay any more. By this time the train had stopped again. 'Hold on, I'll be back,' he said, and shuffled off to open the doors. As if *I* was going anywhere.

He returned a few minutes later after collecting the fares of a group of lads returning from a stag party, and insisted I should pay the difference to make up the full price, which I did just to get rid of him. Yet after boarding the London-bound connection at York, when I explained to the ticket inspector that I had paid the difference, he looked alarmed and said I should not have done so. 'We sold you the wrong ticket. It's our mistake, and we can't charge you for it.' Great. 'Ask for a refund at King's Cross,' he advised me.

To be honest I wasn't so bothered about £2.40, not with my suitcase, I thought, as I queued for a cab and as the fresh London air began to relax me and to reassure me I was back in civilisation, where I wanted to stay for a very long time.

25. Maidstone

Instead of an imposing cathedral,
Maidstone has an imposing prison

I had a publisher and the contract was in my hands. The only trouble was that the book itself was still a few thousand words short. Where'd I go? I was wondering just that when I took a call which gave me the answer. It was Simon.

'Fancy doing Maidstone?' he asked.

'No.' I still hadn't forgiven him for suggesting Braintree.

'Expenses paid?'

'Maybe.'

A Maidstone-based TV production company had tracked him down as being the alleged purveyor of unusual insurances and had asked him to appear on a show called *Absolute Cobblers* – 'a sort of *Call My Bluff*', said the blurb. They wanted someone to stand in front of an audience and explain that he worked for an insurance company which sold virgin birth insurance cover, to see whether the audience found the claim convincing or 'absolute cobblers'. Of course, it's all a load of bollocks, but Simon had accepted the offer of sending one of the directors of his insurance company, GRIP. Since he was a one-man band, this was proving difficult.

'Fancy being my senior underwriter?' he asked. My expenses would be paid and I could spend most of the day researching Maidstone for the book, he explained. I said I would, so he rang them back and said he couldn't go himself as he had a funeral to attend but would send underwriter Bill Murphy instead. So, at 24 hours' notice, I set off for Maidstone.

A train from London Bridge eventually arrived to take me to Maidstone East. I say 'eventually' and mean it: the station's display boards were out of service and announcements were coming through every couple of minutes for departing trains, all of which seemed to be 40 to 50 minutes late.

Not long after leaving London Bridge I was to find myself gazing in awe at another part of the Kent countryside. This time the rolling hills and ancient fields uninterrupted by scraggy new building developments amazed me, and I wondered how Kent councils had avoided the temptation to desecrate the land. I even began to wonder whether 'Garden of England' might after all be a justifiable slogan for the county. So much of the view from the window was like what Hampshire, Gloucestershire, Surrey and Christ knows how many other English counties had been until the last decade.

We caught sight of the occasional village in the distance with little in the way of surrounding smeggy, bogus homes in new estates. Every now and again we would pass a small bunch of houses under 30 years of age whose owners had covered their walls with creepers and hanging baskets. The scale of unspoiled countryside ran for miles and miles and quite freaked me after what I'd become used to.

Then, reassuringly, we reached West Malling, a stop or two short of Maidstone itself: a hideous new-looking ugly grey pointed spire atop a box of a church and some nasty houses. And then Maidstone.

I disembarked at Maidstone East, happy to see that it didn't call itself London Maidstone, and exited the station to take a cab to the centre of town. Silly me. I hadn't been aware that in order presumably to impress visitors that this was a big town and in need of upgrading to city status, it gave a station 50 yards east of the high street the title Maidstone East. The cab driver kindly pointed out the length of the 20-second walk I would have to take before hitting Maidstone central. I had a few hours to fill before I was due in the TV studio, so I set off to study the town.

It was cold and raining, a feature I was told to expect in Maidstone and not just by the weather forecast. What I did not expect was the staggering complacency among those employed there in the service industry with respect to just about everything. I'm not just singling out Yates' Wine Lodge here, where I could only have bought a pint if I'd had a lot of time to waste queuing. No, this was an overwhelming lack of attention to detail.

The first bar I went into was called Muggletons I *think*, although the name was obscured by leaves, real or fake. It was a large grey stone building of perhaps a hundred years of age converted into a pub by JD's, which I assume meant JD Wetherspoons. Chains of that type have sterilised the centre of just about every town in England. I went to the bar and stood away from the No Standing Here sign and beneath the No Smoking at the Bar sign. A barman approached me, and I asked for a pint of Directors. He shook his head, which I thought meant it was not on sale, and he explained I had to queue a little further down the bar for Directors. He was in charge of Stella, Fosters and Best, apparently. So I left.

During the following hour I couldn't find anyone I understood. It took me a full five minutes to understand what the woman in the newsagent's was saying, which was that the *Kent Messenger* was the only local paper which covered Maidstone. Her speech comprised nothing but consonants and made Romford locals sound articulate.

The high street was not unpleasant, and probably hosted England's largest collection of exclusive shops. That is to say it was the largest collection of shops I'd seen so far which excluded any premises which were not part of a national chain. Clothes shops, banks, even charity shops – nothing at all local. The only local business was the newsagent's. There's nothing in the way of individual shops in Maidstone's shopping district that would be threatened by the arrival of US shopping chain Wal-Mart.

I popped into Burger King, where I encountered a local concept of queuing which would make the inhabitants of Romford look positively polite. There were three tills, and I stood behind two others queuing in the centre aisle at the rear to await the first available call for the next customer. Suddenly I felt as though I was travelling in the middle lane of a busy motorway in a Skoda: like a speeded-up nature film of ants, people were dashing past either side of this central queue to put in their orders. So I left again, still peckish.

I wandered on down following signposts which were as accurate as a weather forecast, seeking the tourist office. Suddenly I was confronted by a pub which was *not* part of a national chain of theme bars. Elated, I entered Gabriels of Maidstone and asked the barman for a pint of bitter. 'What *sort?*' he asked in a surly manner only to be expected in Maidstone. As far as I could see they only served Flowers, but I looked further down the bar and saw another brew, which, as it was non-Whitbread-owned, I ordered. Three attempts at pouring a glass later, the barman announced that it was off, but would be back on when the landlord arrived later that day. So I asked for Flowers. Nothing emerged from the pipe, and he stood looking as though he was unable to accept that he couldn't serve me. I eventually suggested that when I had asked if I could have a pint of bitter, his answer should have been 'No'. He agreed, with considerable reluctance, and I left.

Time was passing by and I was in need of some kind of sustenance, so it was at this point that I made the fruitless attempt to be served in Yates', inevitably to no avail. I made my way to the bar, passing through the redwood furnishings decorated in colourful plastic-coated menus which made the place resemble the start of a children's birthday party, and counted ten people with cash in their hands waiting to be served by the one barmaid, who seemed to be about 17 years of age and was moving andante along the bar to retrieve bottles from the cabinets behind her. Fuck this, as they say and as I thought, and I left, reassured that Yates' really is somewhere I shall never have to end up stopping for a *drink*. I returned to Gabriels – I'd been seeking sustenance in this shithole of a town for 75 minutes by this time – and found the beer *still* wasn't on.

But then I turned a corner and felt as one feels on finding water in the desert: a Tudor-style low-ceiling pub which actually called itself Ale House, even to the extent of advertising a wide selection of real ales on the outside walls. I ran inside as Cleopatra said she would run to her death. Unashamedly I pushed like a Maidstonian through the mesh of rain-soaked bodies and umbrellas to the crowded yet unattended bar. I continued my quest to be served at the other end of the bar, before seeing two uniformed bar staff hiding behind a pillar discussing their boyfriends. 'Excuse me!' I shouted. One of them looked at me, then back at her friend, before reluctantly coming to serve me. 'A pint of ale, please,' I said. Without a word she began to pull me a pint of Bass. Alarmed at not having been offered some of their advertised selection, I asked if that was all they had. 'Yes!' she said, as though I were some kind of moron. I paid my £2.40 anyway and sat down to read the local paper. Four very overweight gentlemen in creased suits and unironed white shirts took up their positions at the six-seater reserved table opposite me. If it was a choice of ale they were after they would be disappointed.

The usual emerging threats of hospital closures dominated Kent's press. How glad I was to see that the NHS was safe in *their* hands. Meanwhile, large groups in Kent, not least the local councils, are happily declaring that grammar schools are most certainly *not* safe if they have anything to do with it. Perhaps this is because they're all too thick in Kent to pass the eleven-plus anyway. It was reported that the local Conservative council was trying to gag parents' vote for it in order to aid a swift end to grammar schools. Funny that – I thought it was the Tories who introduced comprehensive education in the first place.

Oh – and *look*! – Maidstone has an 'outside chance of winning city status'. *WHY?* It's a poxy little provincial town like all the rest. Instead of fundamental components of a city such as an imposing cathedral, Maidstone has an imposing prison.

Now Maidstone's prison is a subject worth studying. I discovered it as I was walking along in no particular direction and reached the north-east end of the town, where I followed a long, tall wall dating back a hundred years or so. The first noticeable thing about the surrounds of the place after the imposing walls is that there is a pub every few yards, which is more than can be said for the rest of Maidstone. What's more, most of these were largely still in service. Only the first one I came to, the Royal

George, resembled a Southport drinking establishment. The rest looked solvent, and of these there were plenty.

After the few hundred yards of one prison wall, I turned a corner and saw another wall stretching into the distance. The surviving Kray twin still resides there, I'm told. But then I was approaching the entrance to the prison itself, and suddenly I saw the road was lined with white Mercedes with spoilers, bought from some east London garage. Walking to and from the entrance were women with prams, scars and infants. I felt a little scared but thought I might find a story in the pub almost bang opposite the entrance. I walked in and ordered a half-pint from the buxom barmaid, and as I did so I heard the slamming of the prison's wooden gates and the revving of the engine of a 30-foot white stretch limousine which had been reregistered in 1979 and which pulled up outside the pub. In stepped an evil-looking chauffeur followed by a very short and confused-looking man whose demand for a pint sounded more like a belch. I could have stayed for more, but instead I beat a hasty retreat back to Maidstone East.

The outskirts of the small and insignificant town of Maidstone (and *don't* reach for your crayons and write to *The Sun* in protest) comprise a Surrey-like mesh of new estates, which although monstrously large are nothing to compare with the global scale of Goldsworth Park in Woking – though the building firm may have been the same, for the roundabout-linked road structure was identical.

In Maidstone town itself it is noticeable that the population dresses considerably better than in many other provincial centres such as Braintree, Haverhill, Stoke-on-Trent and, especially, Cheltenham. However, if you spend a while studying these people you realise they are pretty much all due for a large shock such as Woking felt in 1989. It was almost like existing in a time warp when I sat in one of the town's theme bars and read a sign above the bar which read 'We accept CASH'. I ruled out the possibility of this being a joke, having by this time assessed the total lack of humour among 100 per cent of the population.

Back out on the street, I noticed a curious type of queue

leading into a pawn shop. I guessed there must have been some sale on that afternoon and curiosity drew me to take a closer look. The queue from the street led into the store, which was called something like Cash Converters, and not to the sales till but rather to an office at the end of the shop where cash loans were made. Maidstone either missed the 1980s or had forgotten them with amazing speed.

After what seemed an eternity it was finally time for me to head off for the studios, which were a long way from the centre of Maidstone East. A cab I shared with a young presenter who had been waiting in the minicab office for an hour took us past several miles of new estates and through many interjoining roundabouts dating as far back as the 1980s.

I'd been assured I could leave after just a few minutes, as soon as they'd been able to film me on stage describing how GRIP insures over 4,000 virgins worldwide over what they perceive as being the millennium bug: impregnation by the Messiah. First I was introduced to the producer and the researcher, the latter of whom told me he had been a journalist for 20 years. He described how difficult it had been tracking down Simon's company, and the presenter thanked me for coming along at such short notice. I just had to keep reminding myself that I worked for Simon.

We talked for a few minutes, and I ran through what I would say to the cameras. 'We also insure people against alien abduction. Most of our clients are from California. We've only had to make one £1 million payout so far,' I explained. The reporter and producer left and I was taken into make-up. As they left, the reporter turned and said, 'Oh, I forgot to ask – is it true?' I looked him in the eye and confirmed that it was absolutely true, never suspecting for a second that he would believe me.

There was still the best part of an hour to kill before the show began for real, during which time I was astonished to hear people running through the show with their headsets making final arrangements: 'Okay, Madam Tussaud's genitals is talking cobblers, but the insurance guy is telling the truth – is that right? Marvellous.'

It was almost my turn to go on stage and I was led to the back of the set, where I was told to await the co-presenter who would lead me on to the stage. This turned out to be a tall northern drag queen in the shortest skirt imaginable and nine-inch heels. He/she came up just as the previous contestant was leaving the stage. 'Okay, loverboy, are you ready?' He/she then took my hand and held it as we waited, poised to walk on. 'Ooh, you're everso calm,' he/she said. 'I thought you looked dead nervous before.' Why is it that all drag queens seem to come from Manchester?

In front of the studio audience I answered questions put to me by the presenter, explaining that I worked for Simon's company, GRIP, which provided unusual insurances to people with real concerns, and that we had sent Bill Clinton an erectional risk policy with an exclusion on Bobitting. Finally I explained that we also provided a policy for the partially sighted. 'The print's very small,' I explained. This would not do at all – I was not supposed to be upstaging the presenter with humour. So I hung around awaiting the all-clear before being ordered back on stage where I was told to reply to the question 'What else do you do?' with the words 'We also insure prostitutes against backache'.

What did the audience make of it? A staggering 50 per cent of them believed it and 50 per cent said it was bullshit. The presenter, who fancied himself as Angus Deayton, read this result and proceeded to tell those who had said it was bullshit that they were all wrong. In the words of Dexter King's agent in *The Tall Guy* (written by Richard Curtis), it's a dark and mysterious world.

26. Lincoln

Its slogan should be 'caveat emptor'

I had really had enough, but someone in Lincolnshire was courteous enough to ring me and ask politely whether I would take a trip up to Lincoln to write up the city. I was still smarting from Central News, one of whose reporters had rung asking me to turn up in some western town for a day's filming. We had discussed the event, then I had mentioned that I assumed I would be paid expenses. It is, after all, five hours from Bethnal Green to Hereford. I had been out of work for eight months writing this book but Central, the TV company whose staff live on expenses, would not pay my expenses to turn up at their convenience. So when the *Lincolnshire Echo* promised to reimburse my travel fare 24 hours after speaking to the broadcasters of cats stuck up trees, I was quite happy to oblige.

The train from London's King's Cross station was alarming. I was surrounded by people returning to Newcastle with their frightening attire and even scarier hair-don'ts. I went to the buffet and walking through nine carriages did not see a single head that had not been permed. Male or female.

I had to change at Peterborough on to a single-carriage Fisher Price-style train. Suddenly the landscape changed. There was gel in the passengers' hair now, and more evidence of manmade fibres.

Then the Peterborough to Lincoln vehicle shuddered into motion and soon the windows were the scene of boring, flat, endless fields of Lincolnshire. It made me seriously wonder why all those wretched housing estates which appear every few yards in the south could not have been put up here. They'd have all *fitted*. And there would have been nothing of any beauty to destroy.

After what seemed to be a few days on this contraption but was probably just a couple of hours, we began to enter Lincoln itself. I guessed, but was not sure, that I was entering pretentious wanker territory. How right I was later proved to be. Let me explain: what has Lincoln got in its favour? A castle. And a cathedral. Excellent! What else? Nothing, with a capital N. So what is Lincoln? It's a city! It is just a shame, then, that it resembles nothing more than a mediocre town in Middle England. People of Lincoln upset? I hope so. It might actually drag some of the lazy hypocrites as far as their local and rather splendid reference library, where they'd discover a few facts, such as that while Lincoln got stuck in a time warp some time in the nineteenth century, in actual fact the rest of the world didn't.

Even the argument that it's a nice place to retire is a bit feeble these days, given the amount of crime which permeates the city from the surrounding estates. St Giles Estate, the biggest and said by locals to be the worst, is often littered with burnt-out cars. It's the sort of place where they film episodes of *The Bill*. But in a way Lincoln itself is what Cheltenham only pretends to be, with a large number of retired colonels occupying the quieter residential areas.

The centre of Lincoln itself is a disgrace when it comes to traffic, which is a mess. Locals quite rightly complain of a surplus of traffic lights, and they are equally right to complain about their ring road, which only covers one half of the town.

Enough of me rhapsodising about the splendours of the Roman city of Lincoln. Let's examine some facts. Lincoln cannot escape the fact that as it is approached by train, in spite of its cathedral it still resembles a bleak northern industrial town. And given what I was reading in the papers that day about the general doziness of train drivers of recent years, it surprises me there aren't more train crashes on that stretch of line, since the surrounding countryside is so flat and boring.

Lincoln is described by its residents as an island. Nowhere does it seem more essential to have a car. There is absolutely nothing around it for many miles apart from the odd village –

though I didn't have the time to find out just quite *how* odd these villages are.

After my experience in Maidstone, where there seemed to be nothing local in the way of stores, I was surprised in Lincoln at the sight of the first business premises, a Lincoln-based bookmakers. But then I crossed the road into the city centre and noticed that just about every third shop seemed to be a bookmakers.

Lincoln is sort of half-done-up. The pedestrianised precincts join shops which are either very new or old, ugly and in decay. One such shop was called 'Clearance Sale' and at its entrance had a huge display of nodding dogs for sale.

Between Lincoln's market and the new buildings across the precinct stands a building around which development occurred but which itself was left to stand. Christ knows why. It looks condemned itself but survived because someone must have argued that it was part of Lincoln's heritage. What the locals have failed to take into account is that apart from the castle and the cathedral, there is a shortage of attractive buildings in Lincoln.

The centrepiece of Lincoln, apart from the 900-year-old cathedral, is its shopping street. One hundred yards of paved street lead downhill from an ornate ancient archway. It's just a shame the archway's reflection falls on Dixons, Lloyds, Next, C&G, Dolcis . . . Still, it enabled me to treat myself to another Freeserve CD.

My blood ran cold and I began to fear deep-seated pretentiousness in the place when I stumbled across the Cheltenham Arms, an old building which in the 1940s became a brewery, later a pub, and in recent years a theme bar. The landlady insisted that 'theme bar' was unfair, but I consider a bar which has been redone in hardwood and has as many large TV screens and computer games as it has tables to be a fucking theme bar.

Apart from one bar called something like O'Donovans, which I entered then promptly left because it smelled strongly of socks, the rest of the bars are *all* theme bars. This is because three years earlier there opened an establishment called Lincoln

University, which in 1999 held the title for the Worst Performing Higher Education Establishment in the UK. Which is saying something. Nowadays, in late morning the city centre fills with reprobate students leaving passers-by aghast with their slack idiom and general unsuitability to the planet.

Peckishness overcame me again so I went into the market and bought a pasty. It was revolting, but this reminded me of my only other brush with the concept of Lincoln, a flatmate called Phil who shared our house while I was at college. He would make a teabag last a fortnight. Now I could see they're all the same in Lincoln: it doesn't matter what the food tastes like, as long as it's cheap. This pasty was large and utterly unpalatable but only 35 pence. I tried a second mouthful before passing a bin into which I projected both the mouthful and the pasty. A patisserie further along then sold me a sausage roll for 56 pence, and it was on biting into this that I realised Lincoln's slogan should be 'caveat emptor', or 'let the buyer beware': the sausage in the roll didn't just look as though it had spent the last two weeks in a brothel, it was dry and flaky inside a sweaty, grease-lined pastry. I sensed bile being projected into my stomach and ruled out eating again until I returned to London. The local paper, the *Lincolnshire Echo*, had stories galore of heart bypass operations among its residents. On that diet I'm not surprised.

The local yoof, meanwhile, complain about a lack of enter-tainment and the stuffy local council continues to spend money on ventures which benefit nobody but itself and its cronies. Backing up the hideous nature of the local alleged dignitaries is a story I was told in a theme bar by a friendly enough guy called John who hates students and hates the local council even more. He described how the mayoress had shacked up with the council's chauffeur, a detail of salaciousness which vehemently denied until months later when it emerged that the two were to marry. 'These two were shagging the night before the Queen was due to come and open the university,' he said, disgusted.

At the cathedral I learned more about modern Lincoln than I did about the building itself. A local story had broken which described how a party of some 27 French schoolchildren were persuaded that it was a compulsory £1 each to tour the place – the only conceivable reason why anyone should wish to visit Lincoln, which is so far out of the way from civilisation. Unable to raise £27, they left, disappointed. This fascism among those manning the desks at the entrances where visitors are invited to make voluntary donations appalled me once again, after it had happened to me when I had visited Salisbury Cathedral. Fortunately, on both occasions I understood the meaning of the word 'voluntary'. Salisbury never made it into the book because in spite of much of it having been destroyed, life there is a little too civil and varied to be placed alongside the likes of Lincoln and Slough.

27. Luton

*It is such a rotten place, even the locals
have nothing to say in its favour*

I had spent two cosy weeks in London writing up the book before an edit and a word count showed me I was short of copy. Realising I had to go out again into the inhospitable provinces made me feel like a prisoner who has just had his parole turned down – not that I've ever been one, of course.

It had just started to rain after a long dry spell when I stepped off the train in Luton, and the streets smelled of a mixture of vomit and piss in the humid air.

Luton is a showpiece for the concrete architecture designers of the 1950s and '60s, and its layout is largely for the benefit of motor vehicles rather than pedestrians. The way this has been addressed does not achieve much in the way of providing a solution: millions of pounds have been spent pedestrianising the town's shopping district. This is where most people hang out, safe from passing vehicles save the odd high-speed police chase across the paved walkways.

Shops in the surrounding streets no longer seem to get much business, so while designer shops sit alongside national chains in the large interior of the imaginatively titled Arndale Centre, outside the mall just about the only kinds of shops still open in Luton today are discount stores and resellers of bankrupt stock.

The local press has some pretty frightening reports on what the youth of Luton gets up to, I noticed as I read the *Luton News*, 'Voice of Town and Country'. Every robbery I read about that day was committed with the use of a gun, and every crime reported was committed by a young black male. Reading through this paper was like watching an episode of *The Bill*, with reports of gangs of youths making old and disabled residents' lives a misery yet never ending up being caught by the police.

It's the hat industry that keeps Luton on the map. That and the airport. It's funny – you travel at high speed out of London for 40 minutes and get to a station which calls itself London Luton Airport. Luton's halfway to the bloody Midlands. It certainly fooled an Australian woman (not difficult), Deborah Barrett, who in her round-the-world trip landed in Luton and decided to spend her time there. Best place for Australians, Luton is. They'll feel at home, surrounded by fellow convicts. The *Luton and Dunstable Herald* ran the story reporting that this woman arrived in Luton and decided to stay there rather than travelling on to London itself. Luton for a *month*? No thanks. Chiltern FM had reported Luton as being one of the most boring places in the country, and she had responded in its defence. Well, it's certainly bleak. But for the visitor, or at least for me when I was up there, there really never is a dull moment. It is such a rotten place, whose locals themselves have nothing to say in its favour.

Like everywhere else, the only ones to defend the place are local councillors and empty-headed local radio DJs. And besides, comments by Australians should never be taken very seriously, however earnestly they are expressed. (Just to put it into context and prevent any criticism of my perpetual damnation of Aussies, I met some once. Australians, I quickly learned, believe it was their country that invented everything from the internal combustion engine to the cathode ray. One of them I met claimed barbed wire was an Australian invention. I'd no reason to believe it wasn't but I was fed up with the lot of them, so I said, 'They probably had that in Henry VIII's time,' whereupon my antipodean interlocutor rounded on me and asked brusquely by way of defence, 'How do they know he *existed*?')*

The old joke about the difference between Australia and yoghurt applies equally in Luton: yoghurt is a living culture.

---

* In actual fact barbed wire was invented in the US to keep cattle on private property.

Anyway, as regards not being dull, which Australians are, in Luton I walked past the shopping centre, picking up a free Internet CD on the way, and walked out the other end into St George's Square. Ahead of me some youths of about 14 were beating the crap out of a smaller boy, while to their left two lads slightly older were trying to destroy the top half of a council litter bin. It was about 1 p.m. and there were hundreds of shoppers around, on their lunch breaks and/or just shoplifting.

'Your mother's a honky!' shouted two cropped-haired boys of around ten as they jumped up and down on the white stick of an elderly visitor from the West Country. They ran off and his plight was completely ignored by the caring Lutonians who gave him a wide berth on the busy pedestrianised precinct as he helplessly tried to straighten his irredeemably bent walking aid. I considered going to his aid but decided to stick with the principle of 'when in Rome, do as the Romans do'.

Another 50 yards on I could see a crowd of about 100 people standing about watching what looked like three men punching the hell out of another man. 'Don't hurt me!' he kept shouting. But as I approached I saw his aggressors were in fact security guards who were restraining him pending the arrival of two police cars with reinforcements. I looked around again and could see that most people in the town seemed to have the complexion of those who exist on a diet of chips and burgers.

Across a 50-yard concrete town square – or circle – decorated with a few scattered hanging baskets was a café/bar, inside which were exactly the type of people Luton Council clearly hopes everyone in the district will be: simple, unimaginative people meeting for their lunch breaks away from their jobs as supervisors in the nearby shops, or housewives meeting other housewives to hold sub-trivial conversations on the most banal issues. These few acres of shopping space are all Luton seems to offer.

There's no shortage of village idiots in Luton. These people have given up grasping for some kind of hope. One bloke of around 50 in a baggy tracksuit and a torn check shirt was talking in tones of familiarity to anyone in the bar who would listen, in the process getting disconcerted looks from everyone he addressed. As he left after a few minutes, I saw that in his right hand he was carrying an electric kettle, and it suddenly reminded me of Gloucester, except that nobody was trying to kid these people in Luton that they lived anywhere special. Indeed, I saw no 'Welcome to Luton' signs, and certainly none that welcomed the visitor to 'Historic' Luton.

Feeling even less at ease than I had felt in the rougher parts of Stoke-on-Trent, I took a minicab rather than a bus to the outskirts of the town. Luton, I noted, was doing to Bedfordshire what Huntingdon has done to Cambridgeshire, but with even less subtlety: huge housing estates were grimly and rapidly corroding the spaces between the highways and flyovers. I didn't know what was worse – thousands of identical new houses or the ridiculous eyesores of the Huntingdon 1990s mock-Tudor houses.

I moved on to another pub. With hindsight this was brave of me. In there, two ten-year-old boys were fighting over the cue at the pool table. After five or so minutes and a bit of blood, their mother – or was it their childminder? – threatened them loudly, saying that they would get no Coke and chips unless they piped down. To no avail. Sadly she did not employ the cue that she had at her disposal to cane the little brats. They'll be stealing cars in a year from now, I thought.

But the council is interested only in dressing up the town, not in addressing its rather serious problem of youth crime. Presumably because the tourist office in Luton is run by the council itself, it does not have a list of local pubs, as the council does not want to be seen to be encouraging alcohol consumption. It's a funny way of addressing the problems on its doorstep of juvenile and 'gypsy' crime, denying visitors any tips on where to booze. Or perhaps there really *isn't* anywhere to drink in comfort and safety in Luton. 'We used to have lists of non-smoking pubs, but not any more,' said the woman in the office. Oh, so it's okay to drink alcohol, but smoking does not meet with their approval.

Other literature on Luton was sparse, unless I was prepared

to splash out ten quid on a book of old photographs of the place, which I certainly was not. Apart from a couple of guides to walks around hat factories, about all the Luton tourist office had for the town's visitors was a guide to the shopping centre. So we're all androids now, I thought, before discovering that there really is absolutely bugger all anyone would want to do in Luton except escape. Latest figures showed there were 181,000 people hoping to escape (1996 census).

What delighted me about Luton was the fact that one of the most serious problems it has, at least from the residents' point of view, is the annual influx to the town's parks of gypsies or, to be more accurate, travellers. I say 'delighted' because it illustrates the point I've made about everywhere I visited: councils either cause destruction or perpetuate it for their own sweaty ends.

One woman with whom I felt it probably safe to strike up a conversation told me that she had been to numerous residents' meetings with the council which persisted in a policy of doing absolutely nothing useful. 'The council seems unable to establish a link between a soaring rate in house burglaries and the arrival of the travellers,' she said, knocking back a pint of Greene King. 'Not only that, but they leave rubbish and shit everywhere.' I think she meant the travellers, not the council.

New Directions, the magazine of Luton's local Chamber of Commerce, reported that the unemployed of the town are by and large too poorly educated to *find* work, listing widespread speech and literacy deficiencies as well as a basic lack of honesty and reliability – findings about which I am not surprised.

Meanwhile, one interesting and highly appropriate nostalgic article in a recent edition of the *Herald and Post* featured an 80-year-old article from the same newspaper on the subject of riots in Luton. The article from 1919 went on to warn that the motto for Lutonians should be 'Get home and get to bed early'. I couldn't agree more, I thought, as I hurried to the train station.

28. Darlington

Incredibly loose women

My friend Simon had a meeting to attend in Darlington, so once again I joined him to continue the process of arbitrary visits to discover more decaying locations in the UK. I have to say that this task was about as hard as finding shit in a sewer. I had no other commitments apart from dealing with my dandruff, so I just had to wash and go.

We followed the A1 all the way from London – it's the road to Edinburgh – and apart from a few minor roadworks the journey was a breeze. (It was indeed windy.)

Darlington's done well for itself. It was there that the railway was invented and the town itself made sure as hell that it was remembered for that very reason by ensuring that every train heading for Scotland stops there.

Turning off the A1 on to the A66 to approach Darlington town centre, we passed rows of large and elegant Georgian and Victorian houses. This area is known locally as the West End. I scented a rat immediately, and it was no surprise an hour later when I was in a bar chatting to a bloke who lived in the afore-mentioned district to learn that that particular bar was the closest one to where he lived. His home was 25 minutes' walk further into the so-called West End, a northern snobs' district deprived of everything but houses. So publicans cannot get planning permission there. Joyriders can't stop for a drink when they are steaming through the area either, then. Rules like this simply serve to underline the futility of these people's existence. It's all terribly un-British. Except for towns like this, the only place I know in the world outside Europe that exists on a diet of regulation is America. And Australia and New Zealand. But it's not British.

Anyway, drive on through those streets of pretentious dwellings and you reach Darlington central. The first noticeable things you pass are the places that really represent the town itself, for instance a sex shop and, nearby, a church converted into a bathroom centre. It's a widely held theory around there that Darlington is the prostitute capital of Europe. The ladies presumably reckon that in the latter they can cleanse their souls too.

Despite Darlington's claims to a locomotive history, the train station itself is legendary for being hard to find by anyone who hasn't arrived in the town by train. We certainly did not want to find it but through a series of wrong turns ended up driving into the station's car park. Eventually, however, we found the town centre, where I saw the first Christmas lights of the year. It was late September.

This was the first visit I was to make to the north-east, and the make-up of the people was markedly different from anything I'd seen elsewhere in England. The huge tits that were spilling out from just about every girl's top were not in themselves remarkable, but the hair colour of the chicks that bore them was: the majority were Norse blondes, not peroxide blondes.

First stop, a town-centre pub. Unlike Darlington's West End, the town's centre alone has over 30 pubs. It was a Wednesday evening and we ventured into a semi-themed bar. Its special was Best Scotch. Scotch is a Geordie thing. Tastes revolting, stings your lips, but when in Rome . . .

An array of girls was seated around the pub, most still wearing their checkout name badges. This presumably saves time during a chat-up, for which, as we were to discover, Darlington women are more than ready. Indeed, most of them are not merely ready but incredibly loose.

We picked on one simply to enquire about potential nightlife in the town, asking her to recommend a nightclub. Her answer? 'A *safe* one?' Like many of Darlington's women, she was broad-thighed with tits to match. There is something else to note about Darlington's women too: they are either made-up or spotty, seldom both.

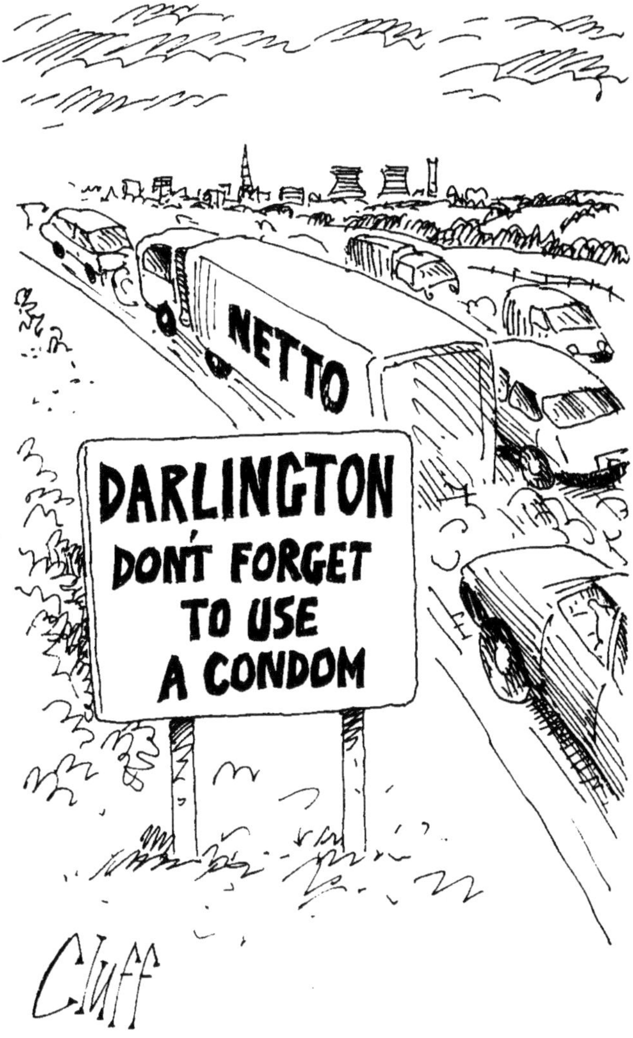
NETTO
DARLINGTON
DON'T FORGET
TO USE
A CONDOM
Cluff

None the wiser, we returned to the bar, upon which was placed a collection box which could have been nicked from a Macclesfield pub and carried across the Pennines. It read, in large print, 'The Samaritans – To Help the Despairing and the Suicidal'. That was going to be us before long. Oh yeah – and there was also a collection box for Age Concern. Concern at the prospect of ageing in a place like Darlington, I presume.

This was too much for us poor city dwellers, and by that I mean city of London, not city of Darlington as it is presumably making a bid to become – something to do with the Lottery or the fact that all provincial councillors are sad wankers. Call me old-fashioned.

Emerging from the pub, Simon pointed out yet another point of ridicule: a Vaux pub which had a closing-down sale. What that entailed we couldn't summon up the interest to discover, but presumably it meant cheap and possibly stale beer.

We had to go on to a place called Number 22, listed by CAMRA as the second-best pub in England, where we were due to meet our cartoonist. The place was incredible, as in unbelievable: in layout and decor it was like a thirty-something bar in Cheltenham only with a greater variety of ales. Still, we were also able to see our first working fireplace of the year. So they get gas up north as well now?

Despair grew and I discovered that Darlington is a Quaker town. It is only a shame that it isn't a Shakers' town. On the contrary, though small, the town has an inter-shagging community. Nowhere is this more clear than in the Imperial Express Café, a 'continental Italian coffee joint' described even by the locals as pretentious and the source of much local gossip. Very Darlington. 'Darlington's a cesspit for having affairs,' a girl whose name I missed told me. 'Our gardener left to shack up with the family I used to babysit. He's now going out with the mother of the sister of the bloke my sister used to shag.' Tongue-twisting in more ways than one.

Darlington is even more repressive than Southport when it comes to nightlife. Fortunately we had come prepared. There is a ritual in that part of the world, whenever discussing potential nightspots, whereby your interlocutor first examines what you have on your feet. If you are wearing trainers the subject becomes academic: you won't get in *anywhere*. Not in *any* of the town's three nightclubs. The only other criterion is if you are a squaddie then you won't get in regardless of how you are shod. An attractive girl called Sarah explained how easily they are identified: 'They're all as thick as shit and you can spot them a mile off.'

Given that these are the only criteria for entry, there is an inevitably high number of underage drinkers in the bars and nightclubs of Darlington. It was shocking later on to see girls who looked as young as 14 strutting their stuff on the dance floor, one or two of them with little school satchel-like rucksacks strapped to the middle of their backs.

The girls a little older than them are on a mission: to find a husband. One candidly explained to me, 'There is a culture of expectation in Darlington. If you have expectation, you will succeed. But people won't move to Darlington to fulfil them-selves.' I wonder what she meant.

We were still in Number 22 and running up a tab. Simon had quietly organised two parties of admirers at each end of the bar, out of sight of each other. Each group consisted of five or six girls, and each was told to put any drinks orders on his credit card, which he had left behind the bar. Rapidly the respective tables filled with empty and half-empty bottles of Australian Shiraz, which suggested good taste in wine if not in fashion up in Darlington.

An attractive and intelligent girl named Jenny had plenty to say about the town. 'The locals think the land is flat and that the world starts and ends in Darlington. A good night out is spending your last pound on half a pint of Guinness in the hope you will win the meat raffle. The reality is that there are some extremely poverty-ridden estates where people would risk spending their last pound just to have the chance of winning enough food to feed their families. It's a very well-marketed raffle.' In Darlington, she added, girls wear fur-lined knickers instead of socks.

We walked into a nightclub named Bojangles and Simon asked to see the manager, to whom he explained the purpose of our visit. He was aiming for free admission, so I explained to the manager that I was the author. He asked to see my press card, which I produced, my thumb concealing the words 'Expires February 1992', and he waved us on, waiving also the £2 entrance fee. He showed us up to the bar, bought us both a drink and proceeded to tell the barman to give us free drinks. For the next four hours, until the place closed at just after 2 a.m., we drank *ex gratia*.

It was '70s night, which was a good start – none of this inharmonious claptrap that one hears bellowing from car speakers in between mindless, intrusive and unwelcome commercial radio adverts to which so many people seem happy to expose themselves. The place, the manager said, could hold 960 people, which was impressive. 'People are out to get drunk and have a good time. Our aim is to get an atmosphere going,' he said. He was certainly doing a good job: not content with just playing Abba hits, he had hired a singing/dancing combo called The Hustle, and the crowd loved it. It was eerie to witness so many young people dancing along to hits their mothers used to enjoy. The Hustle comprised a guy in an Afro wig and sparkling jacket, dancing with a leggy girl whilst being flashed upon by a multi-coloured lighting system.

There was also a mysterious atmosphere of *bonhomie* among the whole crowd. I saw demented, ugly, sad male after demented, ugly, sad male going after single-looking chicks on the dance floor, and not once did their subsequent rejection appear to be churlish. One hunchback in clothes that didn't seem to have been *washed* since the 1970s approached a girl of around 16 dancing by herself to a Bay City Rollers hit, and she simply had to *smile* the words 'go away and have a bath'.

There seemed to be a convention for chatting up a potential partner in Darlington's nightclubs – or at least in Bojangles. Three girls approached us in the space of an hour, each in turn purporting to ask the time and each leaving when we simply replied that we didn't have a watch – and I've never seen anyone looking so dispirited simply at not being told the time. Each then proceeded to cheer up the next man of whom they asked the time, and who on each occasion recognised the mating call and responded accordingly.

At a little after 11 p.m. my senses told me something was wrong. A girl in 1960s swimwear was dancing flamboyantly to 1990s music – at a 1970s evening. So much for convention. But a couple of minutes later everything was back on track as The Hustle announced that the Gilbert O'Sullivan track 'Get Down' was to be played next for Jackie, who was celebrating her 19th birthday. In the words of Martin Clunes in *Men Behaving Badly*, 'Whatever happened to Gilbert O'Sullivan? Nothing worth any *money*.' For any fans, he has a website and plays the occasional concert. Played one in 1998, in fact.

At around 1 a.m. the music reverted to Abba, and Louise approached me from the dance floor to tell me this was the best music she and her friends had ever heard. Louise was pretty but a little on the educationally subnormal side. By contrast, now dominating the dance floor was a herd of mooses, starting at 17 stone. These were the Darlington cleaners, their duty being to clean up the unpicked-up loose men from the dance floor and whisk them away as unclumsily as their form would allow.

At 2 a.m. the bar closed and at 2.10 a.m. the lights came on and the theme music to *Happy Days* was played to encourage everyone who remained to get the hell out of there. We left to take up our respective hotel suites. Mine was the passenger seat, Simon's the driver's seat, in the adjoining car park. To make room for the seats to recline, Simon threw out a few bags of rubbish. It was 2.25 a.m.

I was overcome by sleep immediately, but three minutes later I awoke to the sound of the passenger door opening. I looked across into the face of a policeman who was removing the ignition keys. I persuaded him we weren't planning on driving, and explained we had been unable to find a B&B.

'The CCTV recorded you throwing rubbish away,' he barked. So *that's* what those cameras are for. I had to retrieve the bags and put them in the boot.

Some five hours later, after I'd found myself unable to return to sleep, Simon awoke and we drove from the car park to head for Gateshead. We had gone no more than 100 yards before a flashing blue siren appeared behind us. Simon was breathalysed and the reading, he claims, went through amber and into red. Why did they not charge him there and then? Heaven only knows. Instead they ordered him to get a cup of coffee and not to head off again for another hour. And off they went.

So we found McDonald's and bought a McBreakfast. Darlington's McDonald's was amazing. For a start you could smoke in there. Then, as we were preparing to leave, a waitress came round with a flask of coffee and offered us a free top-up, which I gratefully accepted. Was this really McDonald's? She kept addressing us as 'pet': 'I'll take this for you, pet . . . all right, pet . . . more coffee, pet?' In Darlington this is known as light petting.

I turned my phone on only to pick up a message from an irate producer saying I'd missed my live interview with BBC Radio Lincoln at 8.30 that morning. Pisser.

Simon's phone rang too. He wrote a message down on the back of a piece of paper and turned it over to see it was the bar bill from Number 22. The total he had been charged for about seven bottles of wine and innumerable pints of beer was . . . £18.25. It was one digit short. Apart from the McDonald's, that was the only money to have been spent by either of us through-out our whole visit. So we were surprised to find ourselves leaving with something of a soft spot for Darlington.

29. Gateshead

A crowded valley of deceased industry
across the Tyne river from Newcastle

Mist clung to the trees in the rolling valleys and the windscreen wipers worked furiously as, suitably injected with caffeine at the behest of the Old Bill, we made our way 30-odd miles on to Gateshead. We felt like shit but had got away with everything – drinks, hotel bills and drink driving included. So we felt good. We could even forgive the northern lorry drivers whose favourite pastime is driving parallel to their colleagues at 40mph on dual carriageways.

This light-hearted feeling came to an abrupt end as we approached Gateshead, heralded as it was by the most ridiculous waste of space since the Deptford Dome, the Angel of the North. An amazingly ugly statue or sculpture, it resembles a poorly designed scarecrow with an embarrassing pre-Renaissance lack of perspective.

Gateshead itself is appalling. It is a shithole with absolutely nothing to commend it, a crowded valley of deceased industry across the Tyne river from Newcastle. As you approach it you notice Ministry of Transport-style signposts pointing drivers in the direction of something called Retail World. That seems a great way of reviving a derelict town still smarting from the death of heavy industry: build something vast where the locals can spend the money none of them have got.

Off the dual carriageways and heading for the town centre, I could see the heads of everyone we passed: sagging faces, neglected perms, bulging eyes, fags hanging out of the corners of mouths. The women looked like guys prepared early for the November bonfires. The blokes had a look of deep depression and wore black-and-white football shirts, although I didn't study them closely enough to see which advertiser they supported. Their faces were like lightly grated radishes.

As large as the words 'Gateshead College' were those on a sign reading 'CCTV in operation'. Gateshead property is the most uninsurable in the country.

Earlier that week I had put money in a London parking meter, which cost four pence a minute. When we parked in Gateshead's High Street that morning and I put in the first 20 pence, the meter immediately told us we had two and a half hours – still not enough to make me move to Gateshead and buy a car.

We walked on into the town centre. I tried to argue with Simon that this couldn't be the high street because high streets traditionally have shops on them. He assured me it was, and he did, after all, once live in Gateshead while studying law at Newcastle University. But where were the shops? There were no visible commercial premises the entire length of the alleged high street that did not have locked grilles, bars or boards across their frontage.

The cinema had closed down years earlier and just been left to decay. Not even JD Wetherspoon had bothered to renovate it. A telling lack of something chilled me: here was plenty of wall space on which to stick bill posters, yet no one had bothered. It gave a stark message: there is *nothing* happening in Gateshead tonight.

The only open establishments were bingo halls and amusement arcades. Even the parade of 'House Clearance Sale' stores had long seen no trade. Further down the road was the fourth amusement arcade we were to pass, nestled in 1970s waterlogged concrete which would have been demolished in any other town. Except perhaps Stevenage. Eventually we passed another shop still trading. It sold cheap imitation jewellery.

Ahead was a shopping arcade, meriting the title in every respect bar the word 'shop'. It held an amusement centre and a pawnbroker. Nearby was a shop selling discontinued foods, and next door was the inevitable sunbed centre. It was Saturday morning and there was barely a soul in sight.

Round the corner was a fashion shop called Trend, with a large cardboard sign advertising 'All Stock Under a Fiver'. Gateshead was truly turning into the kind of pain not even Nurofen Plus could shift. Approaching us with anything but haste was a bunch of sixty-something women in lime green uniform. On closer inspection I saw they were in fact in their twenties. They had given up hope.

Overlooking the café we found to arrest the worst effects of our hangovers was a multi-storey car park. It had been built of such low-grade and neglected concrete that the top inch or so of its surface had decayed and iron support rods were showing. Hardly the stuff of castles.

The whole of Gateshead, though, looks likely to collapse. No one would miss it if it did. Across the Tyne is Newcastle, which is elegant in its own tawdry way. At least people there can relate to the concept of self-respect. Gateshead is a town where you can at least understand why they are interested in football: there really is fuck all else to distract them from the monotony of life.

Looking further around the town centre, we arrived at a newsagent's. We were at first unable to read the personal adverts placed in the window for the crowds lingering around them. Eventually the crowds dispersed enough for us to read what was on display. Of 15 spaces for adverts, only a small number were filled, with adverts like 'Wanted: home for dead cat'. Next door was a frightening delicatessen which served 'stotties', a form of tasteless bread roll.

Everyone in Gateshead seems to be a freak, even those employed by the Tyneside constabulary. Two policemen walked past, taking a breather between joyrider arrests, and their hands were frighteningly large in comparison with the rest of them. Later on we discovered that the layout of the surrounding roads is designed specifically to slow the passage of joyriders. Gateshead is the joyriding capital of the planet. Visit the place and you can understand why: there's nothing else going on.

It was 11 a.m. as we crossed the road and, sure enough, a car occupied by four youths, none over the age of 12, raced by with

its passenger window broken. Ahead of us was a massive building which stood out because it was new and which was indicative of lame attempts to improve Gateshead's lot. It was the Job Centre. At its entrance was the town's main taxi rank.

Entrepreneurs of Gateshead have an uncanny way of reflecting their lot in the titles of their business premises. A central café was named Get Fed Up. To either side were buildings with bricked-up windows with no building work in progress. Further down the road was an insurance broker whose counter looked as though it would be better at the money-lending desk of a pawn merchant's shop. Gateshead's average commercial premises are derelict buildings.

By the waterfront across the bridge from Newcastle are large tracts of land occupied not with bulldozers and advertising hoardings as you might expect but with discarded sofas, carpets, bits of cars, motorway cones and bits of condemned building. Newcastle has an element of self-respect; Gateshead is just a neglected suburb. It reminded me so much of north and south London; it's amazing what a difference a river can make.

Near the waterfront was a furnishing store with a window display of kitchen furniture all in need of a good dusting. Even the sinks had grease marks. Across the road was a discarded caravan on the pavement beneath an overhead bridge, and alongside it was a skip.

We realised things were not going to get any better so we resigned ourselves to taking a pint in one of the decrepit bars we had passed. We picked the Central Hotel by the waterfront because although the building itself looked condemned, it did not look as though it was about to collapse, which the remainder of our options did.

The patrons couldn't have looked less prosperous if they had tried. It seemed like a scene from a film about the 1930s Depression. The men were all of retirement age, clad in rags and looking as if they had never seen work all their life. In the corner was a jukebox which might have been bequeathed by another bar that had failed. It certainly came from another age: a forensic study suggested that it had been born somewhere around the 31st week of 1978, this being the approximate date when its seven-inch repertoire had featured in the hit parade.

At the opposite end was a television hanging from the wall and broadcasting the home shopping channel. Simultaneously, loudspeakers broadcast on medium wave some local commercial radio station from across the river. The jingles seemed to be the only sound which could arouse any sign of life on the face of the only woman in the bar. She was 30 going on 80 and wearing a yellow nylon skirt and a moth-eaten brown woollen cardigan. The central region of her head was bald and she had done a poor job of disguising it by tying up the surrounding strands with a piece of string. Ahead of her was a half-drunk pint which at the rate she was drinking it was going to last her all week.

I don't want to condemn Gateshead for the sake of it. It is obviously the victim of the demise of heavy industry so it is not to blame for the condition it is in. But the whole place really is a slum. There was only one place more depressing in England and that was Macclesfield. Gateshead is Newcastle's unwanted neighbour. The people of Newcastle must regret the fact that the Tyne Bridge is not a drawbridge. Across the river I could see the elegant Georgian buildings of Newcastle, the beautiful skyline with the cathedral and the riverfront tastefully invested in during recent years. The people of Gateshead, meanwhile, look like they have visited a Hall of Mirrors arcade and come out the other side. With warts. I should have had my hair cut there that day. If I were to have done so I would have come out with change from three quid. (And free hair lice.)

The local residents take the principle of calling a spade a spade to extremes. On the high street was Done Bookmakers, whose slogan was presumably 'you have been'; next door was Ye Old Fleece (ditto); and further up the road was a Chinese takeaway called Garden Ho. Among the boarded-up shops was Gateshead Armoury. It can only be to the advantage of the town that this establishment is now armless.

We returned to the car with 11 minutes to spare before being clamped and were surprised to find it where we had left it. As we tried to escape the town, falling prey in the process to the redesigned anti-joyrider road schemes, we passed yet more features which told their own stories of the town. For instance, where I grew up we had what we called lollipop ladies. In Gateshead they have lollipop mooses.

Simon, who knew Gateshead of old, said he would drive me to the nice end of town. Here the scenery changed dramatically and I was in a land of boarded-up off-licences and drug dealers. He also took me on a scenic tour of the residential outskirts of the town and showed me the legendary spike upon which he impaled himself as a student, laying to rest his sphincter. Or so he tells us.

Gateshead's outskirts are an ugly warren of 1960s housing estates, and it was among these that we spent a good 20 minutes lost as we tried to escape, although escape we finally did. We headed back south until we reached Wetherby in Yorkshire. Yorkshire is such a funny old place, where everyone takes things so seriously. We stopped at a newsagent's and looked around for the local paper. Simon found it and pointed at the photo on the front page of some guy who had made the news locally. 'Guilty!' he said, stabbing with his finger the picture of a man with the face of a child molester. The octogenarian behind the till was unamused, so I said, 'That guy should be wearing a badge saying "Keep away from children".' I followed Simon out of the newsagent's, hoping I hadn't helped contribute to the death columns.

Gateshead had been too painful an experience to use as an exit for the book, so we stopped at Wetherby in order that I could end on a high. Or so I thought.

Wetherby is a town of such old people, its local paper *The Herald* puts its deaths column on the second page. Wetherby is also an experiment waiting to go horribly wrong. It is nothing more than one large retirement home. Its estate agents mostly advertise houses for sale which are yet to be built, and provided these houses were to be filled by no one but the retired this would be fine. But sadly this is not the case. While it is ostensibly a coffee-morning town, its new houses are filling up with younger people as there are not enough pensioners to fill the estates. In the foreseeable future these people will have procreated and brought up the results to a level where no cars will be safe in the town. It is a pointless experiment. The results are already there across the rest of the country. It must be so depressing living in Wetherby, hitherto a picturesque town, soon to be twinned with Gateshead. There is no local industry but a burgeoning idle young population stealing vehicles because there is sod all else to do.

In the window of a craft shop were adverts for forthcoming events in the town. One was an invitation to Wetherby citizens to attend a talk to be given the following week on 'Digging up your ancestors'. I expected to read beneath this that it was to be a lecture presented by Rose West, but she was apparently not available.

The high street was lined with garden shops selling garden furniture, garden ornaments, garden gimmicks and garden benches. Curiously, there was nowhere selling anything in the way of plants. Every second shop was a charity shop, which baffled me: the people of Yorkshire are not known for their charity. Apart from these stores, the only noticeable premises were Indian restaurants. But there were other stores which stood out in their own way: Touchwood DIY; Touchcloth Dry Cleaners; and the George and Dragon pub, with a sign suggesting we could get lunch. 'Food now being served' was emblazoned above the door and my hopes rose before I realised the place was locked and that sign must just have been the name of the landlord. It was time to go.